Preface or whatever.....

Preface....or whatever this thing is called, actually we'll call it ....hmmmm, "How did I end up sleeping in the back of a 2006 Tahoe at the age of 45". Yup let's call it that. These are called Campfire Thoughts, which are either thoughts Im having at the end of the day, or memories that are clouding my mind with as I sit by my daily evening campfire. See I currently live on the road in a custom homemade rv/suv with water, solar electricity a 32" TV. I travel the country exploring and treasure hunting. How did I come from an amazing childhood, into the military, to homeless, to contract work for other countries, to homeless, to family man, to living on the road. What the hell happened. Well after these Campfire Thoughts maybe we as a collective can determine that very answer. What is the key to life, well I have an amazing keyring but none of the keys fit. Daughters who won't speak to me, a sister I haven't seen in years, a mom that was larger than life to me and I wasn't allowed to the funeral. Where did I go wrong, what was that magic thing or decision I made that turned everything on end. After all that why am happier now than I've ever been? How many lives have I crushed to get where I am, how many crushed me, do we use that as a scale to judge who's right or wrong? Well again let's just see?
Buckle up, get a coffee, or a shot and hang on it's gonna get bumpy.....

"I believe every man and woman should eat pancakes in a place no man or woman has ever gone."
    -Rebel Miner.....

Where's her clothes?

A coming of age story...1989...i was about to turn 13 yrs old...it was an amazing summer as we lived on a farm and had every animal imaginable. I was an explorer from birth so every summer day started early at the crack of dawn as left the farm and into the great blue yonder to find all the treasurers that were hidden in the last 2000 years. Today was super special because my cousin had spent the night. Most kids wouldnt go on adventures with me because most ended with a spanking or broke bones. But at 13 also, my cousin was out to prove he could hang whether we were trapping bobcats or seeing who could hold onto boulders and sink farthest to the depths of an old sand pit lake without letting go. On this day we had our way to some old cabin sunk deep in the woods and upon entry we had noticed an old calender. Now this calender wasnt just any old calender, it was adorned with the most beautiful women we had ever seen...and these women for whatever reason had forgotten that it was picture day and forgot their clothes. Now as a boy at 13 this was the treasure of all treasures. Now it was at this moment that my cousin made a decision that would test the trust and fabric of our entire family....it would turn brother against sister and test the loyalty of our entire clan. My cousin took it upon himself to bring the priceless artifact back to the farm in the notion of somehow getting it back to is house. Under no circumstances would i had made this decision. As a lover of the human woman form as I was, I was also well aware of the consequences of said artifact being discovered by my mom or dad and I was not prepared to end my days at 13. So we made ur way back and begin a long drawn out plan to get the calender to my cousins house. Step 1 hide calender where no one would find it.(under the horse trough) Step 2 recover it when my cousin leaves the next morning (fail proof) 8am the following morning...we venture out with a bookbag to load up the loot....first signs of trouble....as we come around the barn we find my dad holding the horse trough up so my mother could spray it out, now this trough hadnt been moved in forever...my cousin and I stand in a state of shock for what seemed hours as my sister (6 yrs old plays) Now everyone seemed in way to good of a mood to have found such debauchery under the trough....we retreat back to the house to make aa plan. Now I had come to the realization that this was the end for me and they were waiting to see if i would confess, as my cousin decided he had over stayed his welcome and was on his way to his house. There i sat for hours on my bed weighing my options, travel to California and start a new life, confess donate my organs to science, or wait it out and play fate.....i chose the latter. The whole day was pins and needles. That night as I got ready for bed I pulled my covers back and there low and behold was the calender tucked into my blanket....now i spent the entire night negotiating with myself who had placed it there...was it my dad in some weird mindset letting a boy be a boy of 13 knowing his childhood and the discovery of women, or my my mom in some crule "look what youve done to our family bringing the devil himself into our home for a sleepover with the witches of skin and flesh....i spent the next 4 days threatening my cousin to confess to my parents that it was his bad chose and his alone....finally after a good ass beating he decided that it was in everyones best interest to call my parents and explain before the ties our family unraveled into some great civil war....so after confessing to his parents and then a gut wrenching phone call to my mom the evil had been undone and it was at that point that the entire family had realized that my sister had found the calender and assumed it was mine and had stuck it in my bed.....no one had known the entire time...i laugh every time i see dirty magazines in seedy convenience stores to this day.....

Thar she Blows!

It's currently 24° and my diesel heater is acting up. Anytime I work with gas, diesel, propane etc theres always my virgo mind at work in the background of explosions, then they escalate to straight nuclear houses leveled atomic bombs. Now knowing how safe I am my mind always goes full bore on what could happen and it brings to memory me and my mother when i was growing up....we didnt have alot of money and dad was always at work so we had to come up with ideas how tofix things or ideas how to have fun. One story comes to mind how my dad single handedly saved the city of Pilot Point from a full blown cold war nuclear attack. Mom purchased a 3 ring air inflatable swimming pool (popular in the 90s). Now being the top thinker and problem solver she was was decidedto usethe airtank to save time in inflating it. Problem solved! Dad comes home from work to find a nice cool waterfilled inflatable pool in the backyard just ready to soak away all the worries and soreness from the day, my mind fails me but i believe my uncle had come overas well and was already in the pool lookin like a mafia guywith a big ole stogey going. Dad puts on his swimmin trunks fires up a good ole marlboro and crawls in.....after a few min of letting the troubles wash away he says to mom, "How did you inflate the pool?" Mom puts on her I can do anything smile on and confidently replies "i used that air tank right there."...pointing at the 2 tanks strapped to dolly. " One filled the top 2 rings and it ran out so I used the other tank to fill the last ring." Now Im sure alot of you arent sure how a cutting torch works but it mixes acetylene with pure oxygen to a perfect mixture to burn 20 times hotter than the surface of the sun. Yes my mom was the original unabomber. How fast can you put a cig out in a swimming pool and how careful can you exit a bomb. Most kids have to navigate their choldhood without killing themselves, me, I did it with the whole world against me......

The First Boogie Man...

So just had a long talk with a friend on how to stay safe camping in the backcountry.
And he was curious to where my " bravery " came from. Again people ask me why i have so many issues with my mom (who is passed) because right before the end we werent close...which hurts more because we were so close when i was younger...the shit we got into together. It was the fall of 1982, I was 6 yrs old going on 32. We lived on a small farm out in the country in an old farm house...it was friday night super late...dad had gone on a overnight hunting trip with his friends....so mom, me and my sister who just a few months old were sleeping in my bed which was up against my bedroom window...old windows on the coast had hinges on top with a screen door clasp at the bottom.....i woke up to the sound of someone trying to get the screen off and not being quiet about it all, mom yelled my dads name out to see if it was him coming home and forgot his keys...it didnt stop...at this point i have already (in my mind) been shot 3 times, stabbed in my throat, and hung in a tree for my dad to see when he got home... just how my mind works...now as a 6 yr old boy thinks ...there not here to steal, they are obviously sea monsters from our huge pond and there coming for me to sacrifice me to the devil...our 2 dogs were going nuts in their pen outside and at some point jumped the fence and the banging outside stopped...now we didnt have a phone and the truck was parked like 75 feet from the backdoor...i begin to beg my mom lets just leave (my mind lets just freakin move we can buy new stuff when we get to the new home)...so my super protective mom (loving and caring) comes up with the idea that i should go get the truck and bring it to the backdoor....problem being...i can only drive said truck forward, i did not know how to backup and didnt think its the most opportune time to teach myself...so mom says ok you go to the truck, start it and open the passenger door and ill bring your sister and run and jump in and we drive away.....by this point, every 1970s and 80s horror movie has

played out in my head and ive died in all of them..horrifically….now let me give you a visual…6 yrs old, blond mullet down mid back, tighty whities, and thats it…i figured i could outrun the devil worshipers with no shoes….the opening of a 1980s screedoor should be a ringtone…just as im about to go subsonic mom says dont run youll get attention..my mind…yes lets drag this out as long as possible…now i cant tell you what happened during that maneuver because i had my eyes closed the entire trip…truck started, doors open, mom flys to the truck…ipop that badboy in gear and mom says we dont ave enough gas to make it anywhere….so we camped out in the truck til daylight…mom breastfeeding with one arm and dads custom sawed off 12 gauge getem stick in the other….this…this is where my bravery comes from…..

Bitch? Go Ahead Make My…

Nintendo Duck Hunt for bitches…it was 1982…beautiful fall day…our farm had a large 10 acre pond on and we were located on the coast so ducks were like mosquitoes this time of year….my sister was ina play pen outside with me like any other day while mom was working around the house…it was my duty to keep an eye on her..(i didnt know i had a sister until i was 20)..it was rare for me to have friends over so i had to come up with my own games and entertainment…today i was learning to jump on a trampoline that had been ripped all the way across by a slightly overweight hippie lady attempting to show my mom that ididnt need any toys that actually functioned like they were suppose to…(noting that my bicycle had been ran over by dads friends so many times that i could only ride in a 80 foot diameter circle pedaling with one foot)…it qas not uncommon to hear gunfire daily around the area, but today the shotgun blasts seeed close and the b bs were falling on the roof and around the yard…so i went inside and told mom…now my mom was young, very soft spoken, never cursed, super religious woman….now as we left the house the b bs were raining down...seems 3 fellows had jumped our fence and were setup duck hunting our pond about 100 yds away....at this point my mom was concerned for our safety so she yelled out hey your trespassing! ....i think one smarted off like "got it or whatever"...my mom got upset and the excitement was growing strong inside me...(i forseen a phone call to dad at work)....now dad was a force to be reckoned with as i learned throughout my existence......so mom being nervous and scared went in the house and grabbed her pistol....now me at this point knew the situation was escalating alittle past the point i was comfortable with but the excitement was overwhelming....so in her desperate housewife lingo she yells out " i have a gun"! And to my surprise she pointed it into the air and fired it.....now this was my first shootout i was involved in so i immediately begin to assess the situation...their gonna kill us.....what happened next was utterly straight from a clint eastwood movie...my mom wore glasses and was blind as a bat without them (she was not wearing them thank the gods)...as if in slow motion one man stands up from his bucket with his shouldered thunder stick and kicks his cap back and says "get back in the house, BITCH!"....I swung my head as fast as possible to catch my mothers reaction and this is what i saw...her left side of her mouth kinda turned up as she brought both hands to the pistol grip while raising the gun in one fluid motion to point directly at the hunters...her left eye begin to close and her head slightly right and she begin to squeeze the trigger slowly and methodically....after the first 2 shots the excitement got to much and begin to call out her shots like a sniper spotter...ive never seen grown men move so fast...mom unloaded the gun and to both our dismay no one was hit (that we know of)...mom called the sheriff and he came and she explained to him what had happened...the (texas) sheriff explained to her that it is super important to refrain in the future from telling law enforcement that they called you a bitch and you tried to kill them...merely trespassing and shooting a weapon was sufficient this is where in a mere 8 seconds i learned a lifetime of respect for women and to never call one that word. It STUCK....

Time is a child....

Now i know your all use to funny stories or humerous jokes...this is not one of those...so as i sip my coffee i find myself at thought why were the only living things on earth that see 2 paths in front of us, and realize very quickly the path that is right for us but yet we choose the one that is normalized to us regardless the pitfalls we see down it. We wait until were faced with the inevitable guilt that someone like a doctor lays out before us that our multiple path options have all come to a dead end and then in haste do we decide to take all the other paths we bypassed for so long only to realize we dont have time now. Time, such a mischievous child....it plays in our yard for hours, days, even years and we sit idol watching him until he finally looks up from his sandbox and says, "Im going home now.." and then and only then do we realize we should have spent every moment with him, and no amount of negotiation will get him to stay awhile longer....he runs off without so much as a wave goodbye...take this day to play with your time, pick him up spin around under the sun, play in the rain with your time,, choose that path that has eluded you so many times before...and just maybe when time gets ready to leave you can walk hand in hand with him home without a care of the yard that you leave behind.........

Have Wagon will Travel...

What would one do for or to a sibling. Year 1989..Lonesome Dove the most epic movie ever was on TV as a mini series....i took it upon myself to be Gus because lets face it I too have not been one to quit on a garmet cause its got alittle age. Our farm which dad had so named (legally and officially) "Ass Acres" where mom & dad bred raised and sold painted donkeys. At 13 I was constantly going on solo camping excursions for days on end, trapping and skinning hides and making homemade recipes with my camp kitchen my grandad had built me. Eventually my setup got to big for me to tote miles into the woods by myself so dad came up with a genious idea (well thats the story i made up in my head) that i could use a donkey and wagon to get my gear to camp....with the epic western burning in my mind this was a genious plan. Now i had no access to a buckboard wagon but i did have a rusty old radio flyer that i could retrofit to hold all my gear and maybe even do a shallow creek crossing if i scouted a shallow fording sight. Only one issue remained....which donkey was going to be my "hell bitch". Well we an old grey donkey that was as calm as they come and too old for anything but companionship and would definitely keep her cool if i latched onto a nasty bobcat in one of my spring traps and would keep me company as i waited for bandits around the fire at night, and definitely wouldnt ditch me in the middle of the highway i had to cross to get to the creek bottom. Now i wasnt an idiot child, I knew i had to test said equipment and wasnt about to use my camp kitchen in the wagon....hmmmm...now my sister was much younger than me and always up for a quest. So being 6 or 7 yrs old and 25 lbs soakin wet she was the perfect camp kitchen. So i got a good lariat rope for a harness and let about 15 feet (this is important dont forget...PHYSICS) 15 feet from donkey to wagon so as not to getmy sister kicked. Tied itoff to the handle of the wagon. Aight lets do this. So my sister took her spot in the wagon, and i placed a tie down strap over her lap you know for safety (so she couldnt bail when she freaked out). Ok all safety checks in place. Trusty whip up and flick of the wrist and with a nice "crack" and a nice dusty pop and nothin....dang...another alittle more determined pop of the lightning leather and again nothin...ok obviously gonna need alittle more motivation so i gently let one pop off about 6 inches off the right butt cheek of ole grey....now im not a good judge of time, but if you know how a whip works, upon the end of the nylon string breaking the sound barrier it makes a violent pop, then the nylon recoils back....between the time of the pop and the micron second recoil my sister, the wagon, and ole grey were gone. The only thing that remained were me, the whip, and small dust cloud, the uncanny sound of a 6 year old girl screaming and the loud breaing of a donkey. As I regained composure what I witnessed was nothing short of a stampede of 6 donkeys and a wagon going 200 mph over its rated limit. Te entire fleet of donkeys were all convinced the wagon with the siren in it was out to kill them violently. Now mental note, the wagon idea was working even at mach 3. Now donkeys are extremely sure footed beasts and can maneuver with out question..so as the bumbling herd nears the end of the pasture they obviously cant continue in the straight line they were focused in, so in one quick deliberate motion ole grey banks a 90° turn. Now I know most of you have flown kites...that moment when you drag it running to get it airborne... that " 15 feet" of lariat rope reached that turn with the wagon, the wagon left the ground and spun into a spin so fast you couldnt distinguish my sisters head from the wheels of the wagon...im guessing at least 20 rolls and never touched the ground in the entire turn...but when that loooooonnnngggg 15 feet of rope regained composure it just so happened the wagon was upside-down. 10 minutes it took to stop old grey....the sight of my sister was something out of a horror movie...her hair was matted with dirt and leaves...her teeth had so much grass between them it looked like a salad...her clothes had somehow turned backwards and she was missing one of her prized " jellies" (popular shoe at the time)...i felt pretty bad for her but i sure was glad it wasnt my camp kitchen....the wrath that this ole cowboy recieved will have to be in its own Campfire Thoughts.....

My Best Friend & Dentist

I have as long as I can remember been very passionate about stuff I enjoyed ...all in or nothing....it has been a tug of war of my best experiences and worst pains....I dont remember how i lost my first tooth but little did I know it was about to be my struggle with my passion for life. My mom told me a story that if I placed this tooth under my pillow when i slept a "tooth fairy" would come and leave a gift under my pillow. Now as a young child I spent the entire day dreaming of what magical gift I would receive...candy, toys, new bicycle...as you can guess my mother wasnt very specific in which the problem began. Now as I begin to ready myself for this experience, my vivid imagination begin to take root...What is a fairy? What allows this tooth fairy to just roam the bedrooms of children without a knock at the door....Wait why does she need and want teeth to the point she trades stuff for them...By now I have worked myself into a frenzy. Obviously this was going to be a hideous creature that doesnt want to be seen during the day. I made it a point to never show fear around my parents because I wanted to be brave. Well hours passed and I had finally come to terms with my fear....I was a safe 36 inches from said pillow and tooth, where this whole underworld trade transaction was going down...I didnt want to be to far away and be touched and informed I wasnt in the right place so 3 feet felt safe....The door creaked and I could see light enter the room slowly. You couldnt have pried my eyelids apart with a knife at this point. I could feel the fairy's presence as she moved to the pillow. I could feel a cramp starting in my back as my whole body tensed up. As quick as she came she was gone. I was so overcome with relief that I wasnt taken to some horrible fairy trading post that I had completely forgot about my prize for not running out the room in a mad dash to the safety of a well lit room where I could fight her off until dad came. The next morning I woke to find 5 dollars under my pillow. I was pretty confident by now that I felt like I had somehow slain a beast. Now as many kids my age at the bright year of 1980 most of my teeth in my mouth was covered in silver caps. Again we refer back to my passion and all in on things that excited me. Now my brain wheel begin to spin...5 dollars for that tooth? Hmmmmm. Mom worked at a cafe most the day and I was allowed to stay home some days...so with my new found need to have all this cash the fairy was toting around I made my way to the kitchen to get my tools for the task at hand. A butter knife because well who could cause much damage with that..probably gonna need a dish towel...made my way to the mirror in the bathroom and peered into the mirror and gave a brief look at the prize at hand...i spent the rest of the day of extracting all my baby teeth that could be plucked. Got all the capped teeth because the knife edge could get under the edges super easy. After the first few i realized the pain was pretty quick to subside the quicker I worked. If they front ones werent loose a few good pulls and they would loosen up....by the time mom got home I had successfully wagered about $55 bucks and was sitting in the living room with the Sears & Roebuck catalog and a bowl full of teeth negotiating with myself what I needed and what could wait til my next meeting with my adult teeth fairy. The trouble I got into out weighed my memory storing process so I cant seem to remember if I got paid or not....

Where Do I Stand? Well.....

I've never been one to speak my mind on certain issues. Alot people ask me where I stand. With the world as it is today with everything going on Ill try to shed some light on how i view these issues. Imagine if you will a huge garden section in a "big box store". They have arranged all the plants in certain sections, flowers, edilbe vegetables, succulents, indoor house plants, etc etc....When we enter we have 1 of 2 plans...1 to pick a certain plant that we already have in mind so we move straight to that area in which it has been categorized or we just want to admire and choose later so we pick a section and move about. In either of those plans we have pre determined our desire for each section or category but not of the individual plants in those categories. I know it might seem confusing but bear with me. What if you came in and all the plants were placed in just randomness, mixed all together. Suddenly we are forced to try to distinguish which are which. Now take all that and vision this...a true blood biological dad of a child will glady take a bullet for his child, and the same with a mother. Now suddenly the adoptive parent sounds off "I would as well, its no different!". And their correct, its no different. Only they got to know the child thru steps or were placed with the child and told or given a piece of paper that says they are the parents, fact of the matter they still feel the same way. So my view, I believe were all born with the exact same love for everyone here but we let society, rules, government, stereotypes etc devalue that love for certain people or groups. Until we can walk in and just see a beautiful garden and not concern ourselves with the classification we cant love the individuals. Stop thinking about the groups were all placed in or dividing us by what or how we believe. The most beautiful flowering plants on earth all have a day when they dont have flowers but their beautiful none the less and they dont get placed in another group because of it. So the next time someone or a group doesnt feel or believe as you do its ok their still a plant and you can love them just the same. Your all flowers to me and I thank my wonderful parents for raising me to see each human with love and respect. So my stance on all the current issues around the world is this and will always will be "i love ya".....

He's the Best Thing I Know....

I act and sometimes look just like a sasquatch but this man was the original sasquatch. If it happened in nature he knew why and how. He is the reason I explore every inch of this planet like a curious cat. We ran the rivers, creeks, lakes and beaches..I remember watching the old Marty Stouffer show and he would say something about an animal and I would have to find out from dad if he was right lol...we built a house in the middle of a forest no electricity no water but not once did i question if he could...there was not anything he couldnt do in the wild...i remember when people would ask yall are gonna live here? I had so much pride knowing well you obviously dont know my dad....so when i barrel off into the mountains, desert, swamps im pretty confident cause i had an amazing teacher who used to barrel off into them and say come on keep up, and just fyi in the 80s he looked way more like a sasquatch then i do now!! Love ya pops....

Take a Moment...

We all love the Moon and Sun...we gaze upon them both with aww and wonder. We have as humans tried to be close to them and study them. Countless photos of them, countless hours of staring at them during rises and sets. Entire cultures worshipping them both. Temples created in their honor. Our sheer existence balanced in their presence. So with all that, how profound is it to realize that our bodies and our eyes are actually made from fragments of the Moon and Sun, and to be gazed upon by another that loves us from eyes made from both these celestial bodies. So when that person looks at us with love, its the Moon and Sun gazing back with the same aww and wonder. No worries, Ill be back to my smartass carefree self after coffee, but just take a moment today and think about that.....

My Buddy "Tim Buck Too"

It was 1998 I was in the Army stationed in Schofield Barracks Hawaii. I was a senior scout for a Long Range Surveillance Detachment. Every once in awhile a super cool school slot would become available and was almost always offered to our detachment first. Myself and a few others got to attend Malaysian Combat Tracker School taught by some of the best human trackers on the planet from Malaysia. Now I was 20 years old at the time and my leadership at the time did not accept failure as an option, so we went and we gave 150% as to graduate. The first 2 weeks your taught things like how vegetation reacts to people moving through it, like if a limb is cracked how long before the leaves wilt or an ant bed is disrupted, how long before they rebuild as to calculate how long ago a person or group moved through the area. Before long we found our selves being able to just sit for a moment and study a small section of ground and determine how many people moved thru, how fast they were traveling, and what hand they were carrying their weapons in. A few of us had become very confident and built a kind of rudimentary banter with a few of the instructors. Sometimes we would get breaks in the jungle and just sit and talk about the differences in our cultures. Before long it was time for our final test. To be able to track our instructors, who would move thru the jungle attempting to not leave signs behind. Were broke into 3 man teams. Two men who werent currently being graded would pull security for the man tracking, because in real world scenarios not only must you track them, you had to do it and still be stealthy and not get compromised. Well it was my test day, and as luck seemed fitting one of the post acting commanders was along as an observer and brought along a female photographer from the post newspaper. Well my instructor that I was to track was a small man in stature and I knew he would really make it difficult do to our banter that we had built over the weeks. So I knew I would have to make up some time by looking further head for signs left to make up ground to get the point of completion in under the 2 hour window. I was doing pretty well but having the general tagging along made me super nervous and I was sure I was going to make a mistake, and after 2 points of having to back track a few meters I was sure I was behind on time. Now what happened next could only be set in the stars for yours truly....now the instructor being confident in the fact that he had awhile before we gained ground on him decided he had a moment to take care of some personal business in a small clearing in the jungle....so as myself, 2 security guys, a general, and young female reporter broke through the clearing we found before us a 5 foot tall Malaysian man in the process of, well he was going number 2, bronzy ass glistening as the sun broke through the jungle canopy....it was by for one of the most awkward times in my life but I passed with flying colors, and actually kept up correspondence with the gentleman for many years after.....

What Do I Believe In....Hmmmm?

Im not gonna sit here and bore you with the details of what I believe what happens before were born, or after we die. Lets discuss the in-between. We come into this world for the most part kickin and screamin butt naked. Given the opportunity I plan on leavin the exact same way, just with a smile. There is nothing you can do about it, its coming. By it I mean death. We have put such a stigmata on the whole word "death" to make it scary. Nobody wants to die, not even those who chose their time and place, it just seems as though the best option at the time. Find a place in your mental well being to be ok with it. I personally like to look at it like a theme park. Hear me out. So were on a big roller coaster called life and eventually it will end and just maybe theres a bigger and better ride just around the corner. So go through life putting out enough good karma that just maybe you can afford an arm band that gets you on all the rides. And when that time comes, with a big ole shit eatin grin and a loud yeehaw I will exit this ride and await the next. You can take any of your religious beliefs and spiritual thoughts into this realization, so regardless of your beliefs you go alone through that big revolving door but whoever or whatever put you here their intention was never for death to be scary. I just hope its not a quiet candle vigil when i get to that event because its gonna be so awkward when i come in butt naked and laughing like I won the lottery.

"That was one kickass ride!".....Rebel....

Fly with a Busted Wing?

During my Airborne days I jumped out of almost every aircraft and helicopter made in the military from the biggest C17 globemaster all the way down to a smoking old ass AN 2 colt russian biplane Now i was a whopping 18 yrs old when i got the opportunity to go to US Army Airborne School. My first sergeant at the time knew most of the instructors at the school and had given a courtesy call to let them know that a leg (not airborne qualified) LRS guy was coming....so the hazing would be relentless. But I was up for the challenge after already completing the hazing and indoctrination process to get into LRS, worst of anywhere....now what you might not know about ole Rebel is he was a partier, no one partied heavier or longer than me...if i didnt lose pay, get handcuffed by MPs, or get stitched up outside the bar it wasnt a good night. So I was trudging along through the course and already had 2 of the jumps out of a perfectly good airplane out of the way when a couple of the guys and an instructor decided we should go fishing one Saturday. Now I dont know how the rest of the country fishes but apparently in Georgia, they fish just like in Texas with a couple jugs of Whiskey. I dont remember alot of what transpired after a couple a rounds but I sobered up on around 4 am Monday morning with a hangover. And upon accessing the damages I noticed my right hand wasnt working and was the size of a basketball. No worries it wasnt my first injury from alcohol and i could do these drills with both hands behind my back...well thwt was all well and good until 530am when i realized we had to do pullups and i had to pull the rizors on my parachute. Hmmmmmm....long sighhhhh, I got this...well I had a good buddy bunkening with me and we hashed out a plan it was super dark during the pullups and he could lift me from behind without the instructors noticing, this cost me $100 bucks and 2 cab rides to VD drive. Jump days I could merely jump let the wind cary me as it may and land like a sack of wet shit, whats the worst that could happen, I mean if my chute failed i had a good left hand to pull the reserve chute, im golden. 2 jumps and it went off without a hitch, alittle bumped and bruised but was super exciting....1 jump left and i was technically graduated and no one the wiser. Now on this day my hand looked as if i had shoved it down an old coal shute, black as tar so i kept it tucked under my uniform so as no one would see it cause i was not about to have to fly back to my unit as a medical fail. We made our way down to the airfield to board the plane as usual but there had been wind delays so we had to sit most the day....Now what happens next was like something out of an old James Bond movie. The old parachutes from that era were round and had 2 toggles that you could pull down to manipulate the chute to get it to turn...the back of the chute had a missing portion to let air out to give you forward momentum, nothing like the chutes you see on tv. If it was windy you tried to keep your face into the wind as to not catch speed and get drup across the ground. As i exited the plane i tucked my arms in and head down and waited for my chute to open. A good welcoming violent jolt and i was under my canopy, Great! Then I noticed the wind was really whipping and the side of my parachute was folding under the wind, so in perfect situation I should be turning into the wind so my only good hand the left I put my full body weight into it...you dont have alot of time before you come crashing to earth in this style of jumping so what ai wasnt noticing was that I had long since left the drop zone and was over the 100 foot tall pines now. Me still trying to get the chute turned and realizing it was a lost cause begin to prepare...upon my first look down im about 20 feet above the tree tops and racing what seemed like nascar speeds horizontal. One huge step that i had forgotten was to release my weapon and rucksack that was attached to me between my legs. Well should do that now...come to find out a 30lb ruck tethered to a rope around my waist makes a dam fine anchor when it hangs in a tree. I hit the first tall pine in an abrupt violent thud that felt like it took my legs off, then the ruck hung up stopping me almost instantly and taking the wind from sail so to speak, and free falled about 60 feet to my side and hit so hard I forgot i was even in the military...after a looooong walk to the medical truck i was trucked off the e.r. where I had 3 broke ribs, concussion, and somehow had managed to break my hand in 3 places but on that long ride to the E R i knew all i had to do to graduate was literally not die when i landed that last jump....i still dont know if my leaders at the time Travis and Cal ever got the real story but i showed up back to my unit with wings and a cast......

Wait a Minute You Chicken Shits....

The time my uncle broke my heart... I was about 7 yrs old and Dad had bought some acreage out in the piney woods of east texas. No water, no electricity, but him, my mom, and granddad built a nice little cabin on it. He invited the family here, and some of the local people around over for a bonfire. I was a very rambunctious child and was getting less fearless as the years past. I was often made fun of at school because the way i dressed or acted. Mom would layout my clothes but i would modify and usually did recess barefoot. Go figure. It seemed during this time we camped out more than we were in a house, which was fine by me, as I loved to run through the woods and creeks. This party was not unlike any other we had. Lots of beers and lots of stories. Most time the stories were far fetched to try to scare the kids. I was the oldest out of the current batch of kids in our family but had some cousins that were close. The other kids from the area was older than I. We played and ran and screamed up til my uncles got a buzz. Which was normal. My uncles were idols to me because it seemed they could do anything. Hunt, fish, build just anything. There was always respect in our family from the kids upwards or you learned fast the hard way. My oldest uncle was like an outdoors God, like a character straight from the Louis Lamar books he read. He was always trying to test me. So he had come up with a test for all the kids. He told everyone, whoever could go out into the woods and bring back all four of the pretty orange tape from the property corners would get $10. Now in the back of my mind I knew there was a trick, maybe they would sneak out after we left and try and scare us as this was a big parcel and the woods were thick. Or maybe the ribbons werent even there. So as I begin to count all my uncles to confirm they hadnt slipped off into the night I was ready to launch. I ran up and told him to say go. I knew i would have to be on my A game as the 3 older boys was much bigger and faster. My uncle looked at me and begin to talk, Here it comes the catch!! "Oh no!, Your not going we know youll get them." This is for the other kids. My whole world crashed. I was going to shine and show them boys who was king of rhe woods. So I walked backwards and low and behold not one kid would leave 20 feet from the fire. A bunch of scared babies!! I was still heart broken. He long since made up for it as he took me on many an adventure with the killing of my first deer the following year, sometimes walking so far in the cold i just knew my toes and fingers would fall off, and many an early morning boat ride up the creeks to catch catfish bigger than me. He was a mountain of a man both physically, in knowledge of the wild, and in morals. He didnt talk much but when he spoke it was important and worth remembering......

Don't Bite the Wrench That.

So when someone is helping you out, regardless in what way, whether it be mechanically, construction, emotional support, or just a smile. Dont rely on it, dont depend on it, dont set expectations on it in a way that it creates a pretty glass teetering on the edge of a shelf just waiting on a bump. Rigs can be built, engines rebuilt, emotions healed, but for whatever reason bridges are always on back order when they get destroyed. Its ironic to think that WW1 and WW2 both depended on bridges throughout the world. People who help others are usually coming from something broken in their own regards. So when you receive help regardless of what kind its merely a loan of human emotion and will need to be repaid down the road. But the great part is that loan can be repayed in so many other ways. My grandfather was very fast to tell ya that you dont bite the hand that feeds ya. That hand is more than likely gunshy already so dont be shocked when it immediately draws back and is gone forever. If it seems their not attended to your needs it just might be someone else's needs were more important at that time. The universe will provide but not if your to busy pouting to receive it.

"Dont find yourself on an island with all broken bridges and all the materials to mend them on the otherside the creek, cause your truly at the mercy of others to mend them." -Rebel....

Dad was Full of Shit..

Currently camping on the outer tip of the Olympic Peninsula in Washington. Todays high was 59°. I regressed from the wilderness and have spent the entire day going from Neah's Bay, Clallam Bay, Sekiu, and the Makah Indian Reservation going from home to home and havent seen one front door open. Im fairly certain Ive checked them all, even in the rural areas. I have seen some amazing sights. Sea lions, beautiful landscapes, mountain streams, and even as i set typing this on the beach, a bald eagle sets above me perched in a tree, being antoginized by ravens. So after careful consideration, Ive come to the conclusion that either there is a home on the otherside of the bay in Canada with the front door open, with the ac on or Dad was wrong in his logic that you cant actually cool the entire countryside by leaving the front door open with the air on......i know i got a pair of wore out sweats in here somewhere.....

Thank God for Adult Supervision...

No radio will invite visitors. This tale of tails is a more recent event in my conundrums of life experiences. Most of my friends know i love to listen to music when i get up at camp....make coffee, pancakes or waffles and watch the sunrise or wildlife and listen to Robert Plant or Stevie. There was a time when i didnt have a bluetooth speaker and I sat almost perfectly quiet in meditation while eating my viddles. There are many abandoned campgrounds around California. Grass grown up, trees heavy with low uncut limbs, and moss covered picnic tables. I stumbled upon one of these high in the Sierras one day close to the Yuba river. I decided to stay for a few days as it was extremely quiet and i hadnt seen a soul in 2 days. Typical morning and it was just after sunrise when i exited my vehicle for the day. Now im known for attracting wildlife and having strange luck as it may. I made my coffee and pancakes. My mom use to make pancakes for us and dad preferred them similar to crepes, thin large pancakes so on occasion i make them that way too. You can roll them up like tortillas and dip them in syrup and butter. I laid out my morning spread on an old picnic table made of concrete and covered heavily with moss. The lastnights fire still puffed smoke occasionally and gave smell of the fajitas I had the night before. Ive never been a "safe" camper arounds bears, because they simply just dont bother or worry me. As I sat eating I dreamed of the summers when this campground was full and busy of kids running and playing and parents cooking and just enjoying a vacation day. It was exceptionally quiet with just a few birds chirping and I was awaiting the sun to come over the mountain to warm the area as it was brisk. As i leaned forward to take a bite as to not drip syrup all over me in the corner of my eye I caught movement to my left about 30 feet away at the tree line. As i shifted my gaze over, it was a brand new baby bear cub. The hair stood up on my arms as it was definitely a griz cub and this was not good as i was about 20 feet from my truck. I knew if i dashed the startled cub would alert momma and i would be safely in my truck by then. As i shifted my weight to exit the picnic table I could hear brush moving to my right and really close. I had no chance of bailing out of the table quickly due to the design of the big tables of the 80s. The top was thick concrete and the benches made way to close so kids could reach their plates. My big frame would take some finesse to exit and time. I slowly begin to turn my head in hopes that it was the second cub and I would be able to make my move. It was not. Mom had made her way out and she was torn in interest between the fajita smell from the fire ring and me sitting at the table. I did not face her as she was not showing any anxiety at the moment. I could feel her getting closer and her enormous smeller was huffin and puffin. What seemed like hours went by as she slowly made her way right behind me. I could hear the air leave her snout as she breathed slowing in and out. In some kinda of weird almost humorous thought my mind went into somekind of weird comedy mode as I waited for her to hit me with those enormous claws to test me, my brain said why dont you offer a pancake. I almost laughed out loud as the thought why my mind operates like that was funny to me. What the hell, I have nothing to lose at this point so as i lifted the pancake from my plate I could feel the warm breath from her nose on my back through my thin tshirt as she was close and investigating. I lifted the pancake over my shoulder and reached it as far back and up as possible as i had no idea where her mouth was at the time. I had a fading thought of how proud i was that i made moms pancakes that morning and it left about 8 inches of pancake hanging from my hand as in hopes i wouldnt lose fingers in the offering. In almost perfect timing as my hand reached its limit of reach i felt the pancake being tugged from my hand and i released. I could smell her breath, as it smelled of creosote and rotting wood, I later assumed from biting through rotten wood looking for grubs. By this time I had no idea where the cub was and was in sheer panic that if it got wind that mom was eating and came to me my time on this earth was over. And in some kind of magical grace, she walked to my left, past my truck, and and in some sort of comical grin looked back still chewing my pancake, and then off down the grass patched gravel drive of the campground turnaround. The cub had found interest elsewhere and she with pep in her step moved on to keep up. I like to think that it was natures way of blessing me with an experience but i believe she was very familiar with the days of gone when the campground was full of those smells and excitement when she too was a cub and she was also remembering and dreaming of the past as we both enjoyed moms pancakes. One of the best days of my life. I now enjoy loud music in the mornings when in that area.....

Don't Swallow that...

I have a clean mouth. Ive always been pretty good at not slipping bad words in front of my parents or family, but this a tale of a time i didnt know mom was listening. I was about 6 yrs old when i reached the age of i know what the words are and were used for. My mom and dad never used profanity so unless my uncles were around I learned from friends. I was really into hot wheels cars at this age and had built a track outside our home in the sand to play with my cars. I had a friend over one summer day and we were driving our hot wheels around in the sand and created a dukes of hazzard jump. Now my new word was "balls" and away my car flew in the air and when it landed, i gave out a loud and rambunctious " oh my balls!" Because the make believe driver obviously had hit himself in the groin while landing the vehicle. I was 6. Come on follow along lol. Well just so happened mom was in the kitchen with the window open. So the next sound I heard was my name and I immediately knew i was in trouble. Now let me set the pace for you being me in my childhood. Discipline was taken very seriously in my home. I knew what i could push and get away with and i also knew what was off limits. This current incident was a felony. Now my dads system of punishment was his belt AND IT WORKED, but it needed to be reestablished from time to time as i tested the limits. It was also very thought out and detailed like a prisoners last rights. Moms system on the other hand was very chaotic and without establishing a regular pattern. Sometimes i was told to wait on dad, other times i got mouth scolded, and then there were times where i pushed her to far and whatever was close became a lethal weapon of pain. I can attest to the different pain levels of flipflops, fly swatters, short extension cords, and the occasional menu from Dennys. Now mom was very open to new ideas from others but sometimes i believe she lacked the followup of research as in this case. Now i was very aware of the soap in the mouth as it was common for others but i had never experienced it. My personality saw fit that i practice sometimes in the bathtub in the evenings while bathing. I would place the bar of ivory soap in my mouth and set there for a bit. Remove it and think to myself "I got this!" Now as i entered the kitchen my mom was already preparing but something seemed off. There was no weapon and she seemed extremely calm. As she turned towards me she was holding a huge bottle of the old green Palmolive dish soap. Now in my mind im thinking i wonder what that tastes like and how long she would make me hold it in my mouth. As she grabbed my cheeks to make me open my mouth i had a slight sense of wonder, maybe mom was mistaken in the type of soap and i was about to be put to death by soap. As she filled my mouth, it was so bad tasting. I closed my mouth and she said that frightful word. "Swallow ". My whole being was not going to let this happen and before i could run she grabbed me and held my nose. And down it went. I was for sure i was about to die...my throat felt as if i had swallowed ghost peppers. I begin to have the hiccups. And bubbles would come out my mouth and nose. I could see the nervousness on my moms face and then i was sure i was dead. So then begin the water boarding to make it better. It was a long 20 minutes waiting on the hiccups to stop but i could literally not wait on dad to get home so i could 6 year old gaslight my mom. It wasnt all the time your parents make mistakes but this one was not gonna slip by. When dad got home it had to be written in the stars the events that transpired. He came in and was super excited that he bought mom a pistol. Now my imagination immediately went wild. And off we went to go let mom shoot it. So you can

imagine i never quite got an opportunity to tell dad what had happened. And then her first shot, she shot a hole thru a tin can lid at 30 feet. Nope my lips are sealed. Later that night dad asked if had learned my lesson. I simply replied with, " my mouth is spotless dad".
My parents were amazing growing up and the discipline i recieved was needed and looking back made me the person i am, and im grateful i was blessed with parents that loved me enough to care to discipline me. Love ya mom and dad. I was never ever abused.....but probably needed to be....

Muscle Beach Sunnyside Texas...

We lived in a beach town when i was 5...during summer while dad was at work we like to drive on to beach and picnic. Mom and her best friend would drive me and friends to play all day. During spring break the beach would be so packed that you couldnt find parking anywhere....mom would tell me to get out and strut around and the college kids would get a kick out of it and let mom squeeze the car into a spot between their camping rigs....40 years later i just use the strutting to rid off bears, spiders and the occasional older person at the line in Golden Corral steak station. Miss my mom.......

Mind over Matter, Yea it Matters

Great minds dont think alike. I look at our minds as we have 2. A created and a given. Lets start with the given. Our given minds are what were given at some point before were born. Spark of life, conception, brought from a previous, however you believe. This mind attempts to show us what is bad or whats going to get us killed. Babies werent mauled or viciously attacked by monsters before birth, but yet they cry when we try to scare them with ugly faces. You were never thrown from a roller coaster before birth, But yet our minds believe this will be it. Our created minds are what we create to negotiate with our given minds. We ride a roller coaster and create a scenario in our mind that its ok and it was fun. My first jump out of an airplane I could not even swallow i was so scared. Fast forward 10 years to midnight on a summers night 2 1/2 miles over the island of guam. I exit the plane and begin soaring. No clouds, no moon, only the ambient light of the stars and the milky way. I turn myself as i fall away from the island so I can only see the curvature of the earth where the ocean meets the night sky. 22 seconds into this fall I was in the most happiest, memorable, calmest, state of my mind that I have ever been. See I created a mind that trumps my given. My given mind now awaits what my created will do before giving its thought. Take a moment today to just sit and create your mind into something you want. Go on a hike, call someone your upset with and say hi, tell a stranger hi.

Do something with your create mind before your given mind looks at you and says "See I told you so......"

She Scares me Not, She Scares me.

Of all the things in my life that scared me this takes the cake. We do abnormal and chaotic things when were frightened. I have always been extremely embarrassed when something out of the norm happens in public. So i try to stay out of sight out of mind in public places. This day was a nice Sunday in Leesville Louisiana. Weather was nice, and my wife at the time decided we should go out to eat with our 2 very young daughters, 3 and almost 2. The kiddos were very well mannered cause I didnt wanna be the family with the screaming kid in the restaurant. I had just finished a long field medical course in the military. The oldest insisted on sitting in the booth and the youngest was in a high chair. Now this restaurant was only about 400 feet from the big hospital in town but the street configuration was setup so you had to drive about 2 miles to get there. At the time i had an extanded cab 1977 ford 3/4 ton 4x4 truck with huge tires. So we were into our meal and the restaurant was fairly full for lunch that day. My wife said does she look ok? And when i first looked at her it was like she was staring at me but her face was cold white and with out emotion. She was my youngest and all ready a dare devil. She been to the er a handful of times for stunts like running with the metal leg of a swing in her mouth and falling and getting 6 stitches in the back of her throat. At first, i thought she was choking but she was breathing really fast. As i pulled her from the high chair she gave a long a heavy sigh and that was it, she quit breathing and went limp. I immediately layed her small body on the table and cleared the table with her body in one swipe. I tried cpr for 3 seconds and in almost some weird day dream i envisioned her dieing right here doing cpr waiting on emts....so without thought or plan a grabbed the back of her overalls like picking up a 6 pack of beer and ran. I got out the restaurant and everyone just kinda in shock, like no one was doing anything. I pitched her through the window of the closed door on my truck and followed her in. I put the truck in reverse. I thought to myself if i dont let off the accelerator nothing will slow me down. I went over the curb, through the median and into the large landscaped park in front of the hospital. In my mind it was a pretty precise drive. As i came over curb into the ambulance parking for the er a man in scrubbs was smoking outside and ran to meet me as pulled to a loud screeching stop. Now what are the chances that a er surgeon, who smokes, would be on a smoke break at that time. I yelled at him as he approached that she wasnt choking and she had quit breathing. She was the color of a raisin in just the 3 minutes it took to get her here. As passed her to him like a shuddle pass in football. I followed him as we raced to the trauma room. I stood in disbelief as they ripped her clothes off and shoved a pipe down her throat. They immediately grabbed paddles and begin

shocking her lifeless body. My whole entire world just come crashing down. The er nurse tried to make me leave, i put him against the wall and said over my dead body..they let me stay...it took over 4 min to finally get a pulse..i remember waiting to see him say thats it and that the violent thoughts that were in my mind to make him continue...he finally got me calmed down enough to step outside and told me she is stable and we would have to wait when she comes too to see what the damages were. It was then i realized that i had left my wife and daughter at the restaurant. She came too 2 days later and was completely fine. She continued to have seizures for awhile but grew out of it. My wife had somehow got her and my other daughter in the truck..i had no idea they were in the truck i had blinders on. The hospital didnt make me pay for the all the damages to the landscaping. The dr said he would have done the same thing so said no harm no foul. I went back to pay for our meal a few days later to find out that i had threw a wad of money at the waitress on the way out the door. The truck had to have a new radiator and new tire from the trees but it got me there was all that mattered.
Almost worst day ever......worst one is coming soon....

Teenage Mutant..That Will Be $.50.

The 6 yr old poacher. 19 and 80. We lived on a pretty big farm on the coast which was in a few of the other Campfire Thoughts, down on the coast of Texas. I was a wild child in the summers, no shoes, go figure, no shirt, just shorts. I never had a curfew or was ever told to go to bed. I played so hard I was out like a light by 9pm anyways. I dont remember ever having to tell mom or dad where i was headed. Just be home right after dark. Ive always been infatuated with nature. I would have 3 or 4 snakes in my pockets and always trying to catch something. Now Im not trying to talk myself up but I was very savy for 6 yrs old. I noticed the turtles out in the pond would slide off the sides of an old log in the same spots when i ran out there and scared them. So I put my thinkin cap on and grabbed 2 milk crates and some bailing wire and away I went. So I swam out one at a time, and tied the milk crates just below the water line where the turtles would slide right into them when im scared them off. After an hour or so a few climbed their way out on the log and I sprang from the bushes and right into the crates they went. I was a genious I thought to myself. After a long day I had every size turtle imaginable. Now another thing that I was good at was makin money for G.I. Joe toys. I had a dream of owning everyone of them. I would do just about anything for a dollar bill. So after going to the fair a few months prior they had a stand that if you rung a ring around a plastic ducks neck with a ring you got a pet guinea pig. Well I didnt have a stand but I did know how to write some what. So I grabbed an old board slat from my bed and proceeded to spell out pet turtles for 50 cents, and away I went with a huge trash can full of turtles, all kinds and sizes. I got down to the corner of the old highway and set my sign up on the olf fence and even set a few out for display on a string. Now I was doing pretty good, even had a lady buy 10. I was kicked back lost in a day dream of all the toys I would buy later that day when a bright shiny new truck pulled up. He was obviously important fella, cause he had a gun and a badge, but he didnt look like the police I seen around. He slowly walked over and asked to see my merchandise. Well even cops have kids who need pet turtles. He pulled a few out and asked where I had got them. Well i told him my story. He laughed a bit and asked where I lived. Now when big people asked where I lived I got wise quick that I was probably in trouble. So I slowly pointed down the road, tryin to make it look really far in an attemptt to persuade him that it was too far to walk. He ask my name. I told him. He said well Mr Lawson, what we have here is 3 felonies. See you have caught these here turtles illegally without a license, selling property of the great state of texas for profit, and transporting wildlife without a license across the county line. See thats the county line right there and Im an officer with the state of texas fish and game, and I got a call that you were down here selling turtles. Usually about this time i was half way into

making up my story of how to talk my way out of trouble. But dad had got hit not long before having a pet owl and it didnt go well. So i was allready about 12 years into my prison sentence when he said I would have to load and go with him. So i preceeded to explain to him that the house was actually much closer than he thought, and i could just simply go let these turtles go. Nope he wasnt buying it. So we loaded up and away we went. As we pulled up into the yard I had high hopes my loot might somehow ease my parents mind knowing im gonna be incarcerated for awhile. My mom came out and met him in the driveway. They talked for what seemed hours. He came to the door and let me off with a pardon from the governor because I had so much ingenuity in catching them. I couldnt wait to tell my grandpa.
Yall dont tell anybody but I kept the turtles......old house is still there today...but not much longer.....

Get Lost! I Already Am.....

Sometimes being right is wrong. Along about 2010 i got a wild hair to build an airboat. So i droveover to florida an bought an airboat hull off an old guy for a few 100 bucks and brought it back to texas. I dropped a rebuilt 350 chevy motor in it, foulda nice wood prop and run all the systems. Over the next few months i enjoyed all the backwaters texas has to offer. It was straight piped so you could defihear me coming. One particular christmas day i decided to do alittle duck hunting from the boat. I launched from the gravel road i was at and drove it down the little trail to the lake i was on. This area had been in a huge fight over jurisdiction from the county and corp of engineering. The area in question was a strict line where you could hunt and not. I did not want to be in trouble so i made sure i knew where i was at. I was enjoying the cool morning sitting in my boat and i could see a gentleman walking down the hill towards me. The area was all marsh with brown vegetation floating on the water.

There was no way he was gonna make it. Then i noticed it was a game warden. Well i watched as he got about 100 yards away and fell thru the thick vegetation and into the frigid water. He quickly sprang up and out. I yelled if he was ok and he motioned me over. So i packed everything up and headed his way, but not before snapping a pic in secret of him standing there all wet. I had no idea how much trouble that pic would cause. So i fired the old 350 up and it barked and i floored it to get the boat up on plane and across the vegetation and swooped over to him. I could see he was extremely pissed off. He proceeded to tell me that i was hunting in prohibited waters. I knew better than to argue with him as he was very fiesty. So i tried to explain where we were on the map and he wasnt having it. So i offered him a ride back to his truck in which agreed, so away we went. Then just when i thought we were good he wrote me a ticket for poaching, taking resources without permission. I had in the back of my mind ill fight it and be fine. So we went our seperate ways. So on the court date I showed up and asked for a jury because i went back and took photos of the entire area to prove i was right. The judge pulled me aside and said they dont have a jury ready and if i was to loose it could mean prison time. I told him my confidence in where i was. Ive literally spent my entire life leading soldiers all over the world at night to pin point locations, this was day time and with a map, and i had photos. Well he said ok and dropped the case. I left thinking it was over and it was done. A week later i was at work and caught the game warden walking up in the corner of my eye. He didnt say a word, threw me to the ground, handcuffed me, and read me my rights. Then he told me just because they dropped the case it wasnt over, he said he changed the ticket to a felony charge of poaching and trespassing. So away we went to county jail. So after 24 hrs i posted bail. So i decided to twlk to his supervisor as he was a young guy and obviously on a power trip. So i called and asked for a meeting in which he agreed. So i drove to Ft Worth to the state game office. He was an older man with a nice sense of humor. I told him my case and showed him the pictures. He said well lets see what he says. I had no idea he had called the guy in for the appt. He was so mad and looked at the pictures for 1 second and said we were 3 miles down the lake at a different bend. So i reached into my pocket and pulled out the bomb. I said this is you when you fell in and i picked you up. And as you can see thats where these pics were taken. The older gent said well slick seems hes got ya over the pickle barrel. I could see the fire brewing inside him. Then the gent proceeded to tell him right there in front of me he would no longer work for the texas fish and game. He told me he would take care of the charges and apologized and i went on my way. As i left i remember grinning like I accomplished something but then thought if I hadnt taken that picture of him I might have went to prison for a long time.......

Kids Don't Do Drug.....

The Magic Rope. I spent my best days in the military in Long Range Surveillance Detachment. We were a small 6 man team of American Badasses. Trained to operate deep behind enemy lines and do the work before the days of the drones. I had put in my time and training and worked my way up to the coveted Senior Scout position. I was responsible for getting the team to the rear hide sight where the communications were set up and then take the other 2 team members further to the main hide sight. I at 19yrs old would brief chopper pilots in their 30s where we would fly and land. I had to memorize all the gps coordinates in my head of every point in the mission incase of capture the enemy would not get any intel. We would either get deployed by parachute or by Fast rope, basically a thick rope like a firemans pole out of a helicopter., and we would slide down due to the helicopter couldnt land for the terrain. Upon completion we would get picked up by another rope, it would hang below the helicopter and the pilot would hover above the trees while we tied in. And then lifted back to a safe landing zone. Pictures below for reference. This night we were training in Louisiana and we had got picked up by the rope, being the senior scout i was always first out and last in, so i was the bottom man on the rope. We were enjoying the breeze in our faces and the relief of all the combat load off our feet and just swinging way up in the night sky. I have my radio on my ear so i can hear the crew chief and vs so we can communicate with the pilot as he cannot see when we leave or touch the ground. So we were just about to land and the command was 10 feet from the ground, 5 feet, 1 man down 2 man down etc until the entire team was on their feet and we begin hastily removeing the 2 points of linkage from the rope so the helicopter can then break from its hover and leave. Well me being first down, i had my snaplinks undone in a second and begin to help the second man. We have night vision on but with the dust created from the helicopter above us its very hard to see. So as i wrestle my teamamtes snap link he instantly dissappears. The whole team is gone!! Im standing solo on the old runway by myself. I hear the helicopter flying with alot of throttle. My first thought is the bird is going down and their all attached. So i immediately give chase, but I cant see anything as the chopper goes down just a huge dust cloud. As i get closer i drop my gear so i can run faster. Still no sign but the engine sounds good so no horrific crash. As i begin to close on the chopper i begin to see movement on the runway. Its my team. Their all down and tangled in a mess of combat gear rope weapons and moans. Next thought they all fell here. So i begin to attempt to undo them and realize they werent dropped but drug alittle over a footballs distance down the runway which was made of asphalt. The dust begin to clear so i could make out figures in the door of the helicopter. So got everybody untangled and accessed wounds, which no major ones. Alot of bumps bruises, torn off fingernails, but just overall banged up. The pilot while hovering experienced brownout, where the dust cloud consumes the choppers field of view and he becomes disoriented and without notice flew forward and away from where he thought we were and landed. Later that night we laughed and joked about it, and how I the one that usually gets all messed up came out clean as a whistle. The next nights mission i dislocated my shoulder......

The Werewolf of Honolulu...

  I had a pretty awesome childhood growing up but once I got in the military and got paid to do what I loved, my love for alcohol and partying would grab hold and would turn me into a creature of the night. I got stationed in Hawaii right out of bootcamp. I quickly learned where the nightlife never ended, Waikiki Beach. The bars and clubs never closed. You could party as much and as often as you liked. I also quickly learned when the police picked my up they would take me to the mp station and drop me. So I became what was called the runner. I was in extremely good shape and knew all the good hiding spots. So when the bicycle cops would show away i went, i would lead them down the alleys and beaches and into the jungle I would go. Once i hit the jungle I was home free. Then around 10am I would awake from a drunken slumber somewhere in the jungle and make my way back to town. Most of my buddies would either passout or go back to the barracks around 2 am so I would continue to party and then slowly make my way to Dennys located in one of the big hotels. After awhile I made friends with a few ladies of the night who also came to Dennys. One working girl was also from Texas so had a bond and would talk about our nightly exploits. She paid a local limo driver to tote her around town to do her "business". So she would drop me at the barracks on her way home. Well this night was no different from the rest but I had made a wrong turn down an ally and the bicycle cops had me cornered, they hated G.I.s. So away we went down to the mp station. Now I knew the trouble would be bad, probably lose some pay and probably lose my rank due to the times I had got picked up. I had no idea how the morning was about to unfold. The MPs were no different from the local police they also hated us grunts. As we walked down to the drunk tank I noticed a familiar face. It was my platoon Sargeant at the time. Whhhaattt. What had this guy done to be in here and also im done now, because my team leader wont be able to hide this from him now. See a platoon Sargeant was to be respected and you didnt just have a casual conversation with one. As i sit there beside him he asked what i had done. So i told him that i was down on the beach drunk and the cops dont like us down there early in the morning and they pick us up. But i ran. He laughed and begin talking like we were buddies. He told me of the responsibilities he had and how hard it is being married and said this will be the end of his career for sure. He had got into a brawl at a local bar. Well i knew when the change of guard came they would lead us out to the car and drive us to our unit cq desk to have them sign for us. So i said i have a plan, are you in the condition to run? He said what i said just follow me when we get outside the compound. So as we walked down the sidewalk toward the parking lot I sprang our plan into action. Away we went. Around the compound, up the hill, and out onto the street between the buildings. They 2 mps had no chance of keeping up with us as we were fit creatures and could run all day if needed. They soon lost interest and were on their radios, so ai led him into the jungle above town. There was a pay phone close but he encouraged me that if we called someone, someone would find out, so i assured him this phone call would not end like that. So we waited silently in the edge of the jungle. Out of the night a long black limo pulls up and my friend arose from the sunroof and motioned us over. The ride back to base was almost surreal as I sat listening to them talk thinking this larger than life man who had stormed a compound in Panama with the 75th Ranger Battalion was sitting here with me and a lady of the night who became one of my best friends who I still laugh and cut up with today. She and I were just two kids doing what we could to make into this game called life. She dropped us off outside the gates at post and we snuck back on base and never spoke of the incident again. I had a whole new respect for him after that and I really cutback on all the partying....for awhile......

I Made a Pretty "Good" "Bad" Guy....

Ft polk Louisiana is a massive training areas for units to work on the combat skills. No detail is left out from civilian towns with working functioning stores, to chuches being conducted. Actors of all types are portrayed. Everything is simulated from arms deals to gorilla warfare. I at the time was tasked as bad dude who ran a town, kinda like a drug lord. The unit that was there doing their training was the 101st airborne. My task was to disrupt and take out as many convoys as possible. Everyone used simulation rounds which were basically like lasers but with with blank rounds fired. Once initiated the entire area the size of new jersey was an active war zone. So i took my team out, we had an old chevy blazer and civilian clothes. I decided our best bet was to start on the highway while they were all in line at night so it would be hard for them to be able to see whats going on. We took some old barrels and placed in the road and pulled the blazer beside it like a roadblock. The plan was to take out the first vehicle. So a few hours later here they came all in a single line bumper to bumper with no lights. No no no. They were all wearing night vision. So i waited until they got close and stopped and cut the headlights on. I could hear blinded by the lights playing in my head. The passenger of the lead vehicle got out and approached still wearing his night vision like an idiot. Knowing he couldnt see squat with the headlights in his face i walked up stuck my pistol to his chest and said if you move your dead. This was too easy. Then i noticed his rank. He was a capt. I asked if he was in charge of the convoy and like a kid stealing candy he told me yes. So i gathered my team and we slowly approached the vehicle. Nobody but the driver was with him. So we all loaded in his vehicle and i told the capt to radio all clear and to move out. I drove the entire convoy down and a dead end road, 21 vehicles to include their entire mess hall, aid station, and water purification unit. I made him order them all out and tell them we were in a religious sight that doesnt allow weapons. He then ordered them to exit their vehicles without weapons and form up. We, 4 men took prisoner 130 soldiers without a single shot fired. Rules of the game at this time from the observer controller, the high ranking referee, said to execute them all. That capt got his entire unit killed. So away we went for the next convoy. This one would not be so easy as it was mps so we thought. We did the same scenario but this time 6 men exited to approach. As we stood talking in front of the humvee they exited, the driver of the vehicle was still sitting in the driver seat. We were working out a deal to have them pay us to continue down our highway. They were negotiating with their commanders over the radio....i slowly backed up and raised my rifle and fired one shot at their leader about 10 feet away. As the others begin to scramble to get their weapons up the driver who cant see anything just floors the accelerator on the humvee and flys forward running all of us over. I was thrown from the front by the brushguard. The humvee continued for another 1/2 mile before stopping.. it was utter chaos. My team begin trying to get the men accessed for wounds while i struggled to my feet. My hip felt as if it was gone. I limped to the others and sent the oc to call a real world medavac. 3 of the men were ok just banged up really bad but the commander was drug by the vehicle the entire way and was not doing good. I called in a helicopter with smoke and flares and got him evaced. We went to the hospital to see him, and he was in good spirits. Was even laughing about having to now find a driver he could trust if the shit ever hit the fan. When i asked the driver what he was thinking, he replied that we shouldnt have had the headlights on because it blinded him with the night vision, i explained to him that over the next few days i would go ahead and notify the rest of the world that when we get there dont use their headlights at night, and that maybe instead when your driving a 4 billion dollar armed to the teeth convoy, you just keep on going. I truly hope that training helped all those men and women to make better choices later on. I learned alot myself......

Gone Girl....

Gone Girl.
At the end of my first marriage I was about as close to just calling it quits as I've ever been. Seemed there was no clear sight to the end and what was there anyways. I had been going to the bar as much as I could because well lets face it, alcohol makes things go away briefly. I was one of the funniest drunks ever. I had mastered being drunk and was the life of the party. If I was sober I really didn't know how to function in society. Well this night wasn't any different from the rest. I was out enjoying dancing and drinking and just high on life. I remember someone yelling at me and telling me my wife was in the parking lot tearing out my seats with a knife. Well good ridden, I didn't need them anyways. She liked to try to get at me the best way she knew how, because I wouldn't stay home and argue. It never led to anywhere so why do it. I knew deep down it was about over but my personality enabled me to block out the details that were coming. So eventually she went home and parked up at the grocery store and called it a night. The next day I came in about 7 am and told her I was headed to a buddies to help him bale hay on his farm. She had it in her head that I was cheating on her, but couldn't be further from the truth. I just liked to dance. So away I went. My buddy lived down in Southern Louisiana on about 100 acres. He and I was buddies back in LRS together and had some challenging times together in that hardcore unit. So we liked to hangout and reminisce of those times most didn't understand. I had stayed baling hay until alittle past dark and

headed home. I was about to have my worst day ever. I pulled in to my drive and a strange truck was there. First thought was a friend. When I walked in it was my wife's dad. There was nothing, not so much as a picture in my house. She walked out from the back and said these, ill never ever forget them. "Go tell your kids bye because you'll never see them ever again." See she, her dad, and even my own dad had came up with a plan to "rescue" her from the bad man. My dad had rented her a storage unit, and her friends helped her move everything except the water bed out into storage. She even took my socks, uniforms for my work in the military, and the toilet paper. The only reason she left the water bed is because they couldn't figure out how to drain it. Her dad had drove for 9 hrs straight to pick her and the kids up. So I didn't say a word and went to the backyard swing where my kids sat ages 4 and 2. Me and my oldest talked for a bit and I tried to keep my emotions at bay and she finally came around and away they went off into the dark as the taillights faded I thought to myself, how many country songs had just came true. I went to the truck and grabbed my spare tire out of the bed and threw it in the living room and cried for what seemed like hours. I thought about calling my dad but the betrayal was to much to bare. My buddy showed up and we went down to the local Cafe and bought a late night breakfast. I had to go to work in civilian clothes for a week until my attorney finally got her to release my uniforms and vinyl records so at least I'd have music.....she always, well my entire family always thought I was cheating on her, could not be further from the truth....a friend brought a date he had over a few weeks later...she and I would end up falling in love......

Let's get ready and Dive Right into Volume 2....

20 and Divorced

Well we left off in Volume 1 with a mysterious woman that I was soon to fall in love with. As prior known I was a partier, anything and everything revolved around alcohol. I frequented a club off base known as Toon Town. This club was amazing for me because I was freshly divorced, strapped for cash and the women who also were regulars enjoyed the company of a country boy who could dance. On Thursdays they had what was called beer bust. For $13 bucks you purchased a red solo cup at the door and drank as much as you could get down your gullet. I was a professional drinker and knew how much to slam to get my personality on its A game and then place the drinking on cruise control the rest of the night. I had noticed this tall dirty blonde a few times with amazing curves. I never was one to ask for a dance, they just came to me and it worked for my shyness. I had wanted to talk to her alot but just never jumped on the occasion. I was currently dating a lady that also knew how to dance so it was working out. After my divorce I rented a really run down trailer in a trailer park just off base. It was the perfect bachelor pad for me and my buddies. The lady I was with asked if she could crash at my place due to her car was acting up. I was born in a barn but it wasn't at night so I knew what this meant. So after closing down the bar we loaded up and headed to the trailer with a few friends in tow to continue the party at the trailer. On the way a few branched off and it was just my lady and a couple behind us. As we got to the trailer and begin to go inside, I was slapped in the face by fate to realize that my buddy had scored a date for the evening. It was the tall blond. We made eye contact and I was smitten. She was amazingly beautiful in the porch light. So we begin to have a few drinks and my lady and I retired to the room. I couldnt help think of what they were doing in the room down the hall. It wasn't like a jealousy thing, but curiosities. Was this a one night stand for her? Did she frequently do this? What was she like? As the evening progressed I was busy doing what I loved to do, frolicking in the bed. We were having a pretty exciting night so I decided to add alittle humor and fun so I went out to get my bullriding spurs hanging on the lamp in the living room. I had no idea they hadnt made it to the bedroom but was still in the living room. No lights were on but you could definitely see. I was in my birthday suit and so were they. So trying to not make it awkward I just told them I needed these as I reached for the spurs. Well I caught the light just right. I could see her whole silhouette and she was gorgeous. Well in my attempts to see her I caught the lamp cord wrong and it shorted out on the spurs and lit my ass up. Nice light show and alittle dance as we all laughed and giggled. And away I went. The next morning we all went our seperate ways and I asked my buddy about her. Ya know how serious was it? Those kind of questions. As the explanation progressed I remembered he was still married. Oh no I thought in my mind but was also alittle excited because maybe this was a one time deal. So he reassured me it was a one time deal and I asked his permission to pursue her. It was a HUGE no no in the military to go behind a buddies back. So he gave me his blessing. So I spent the next 7 days weaseling my way out of the other ladies eyes and found out she was married anyways. I use to think how crooked this world is, it's like nobody has loyalty anymore and spoke out loud to myself, "Your the worst one!"....then I begin to talk myself into the notion, that I wasnt. I couldnt wait for Friday night. I had so many lines qued up. It was gonna be perfect. Friday came and left, Saturday came and left, no blond anywhere.....Sundays was a recover day for me, lots of water and pizza. About lunchtime I was eating some pizza trying to see how much money I spent and see if I was gonna have electricity or food, when a knock on the door. Who was here, probably a buddy wanting to go fishing. So I swung the door open and to my surprise there she was, my princess in all her wonder, glowing in the sun. Im not 100% sure what she said because I was still in shock. But she again tried to explain that she had lost a shoe in the trailer and decided to stop by to recover it. I said I don't think so, and then immediately realized this was my chance and said come in lets look!! She came in and said it was probably under the couch. Sure enough it was there. Damn, I thought, she really did come for the shoe. So I asked if she would like some pizza and a drink? She agreed. This was it, I had to spring into action stone cold sober. I thought to myself this will never happen. As we sat in awkward silence, she began to talk. She confessed that she left the shoe under the couch on purpose to be able to stop back by. That she used my buddy to meet me but realized at the last minute that I was with someone. Then said she had to build up the nerve to come over. So we talked the rest of the afternoon and all that I tried to tell her about how I was smitten by her, probably fell on deaf ears because she had made the first move. I told her about why the other lady had stayed the night that night and she looked at me and asked if she could stay because hers was acting up as well. We both laughed and had an amzing night that would last over 6 years together.......we'll call her M for the rest of the stories.....you will eventually grow to love her like I did.....

Purgery or Plead the 5th.

I had just finished up kindergarten and I was basically ready for life, I mean I had won the art contest and was the fastest kid in the county and had several ribbons to prove it, well barefooted anyways. My parents had somehow by chance met our next door neighbors who had became the best of friends. They would continue the friendship and are still friends. They swapped paychecks to pay each others bills between paydays, they camped together frequently. If you found one couple you found the other one. Now this couples kids were just almost perfect for me. Their oldest daughter was almost same age as me and we got along great. Notice I said almost. They had a son who was crawling and his mouth was lined with what only could be surgical razor blades. He could bite like a south Texas snapping turtle and no amount of struggle or lightning could get him to release. I was an only child of the family at the time. My mom was much older than her brothers who she helped raise. So I, in theory was a practice kid. Dad & mom were both kind of finding out the ins and outs of raising a wild child. Now when I was told to do something I either done it or not but I remembered being told. Well long poker nights in the house would come to an end and my fingers and arms would be covered in teeth marks from playing with the knife teeth animal and his sister. Finally dad had

had enough. "Son the next time just hit him." Now being older now I know what he meant, but at the time it was a free pass. I couldn't wait for the next opportunity to get my vengeance. So a few nights later, I lay wait with my toys strategically placed around the room. His sister came in and we started playing I waited patiently for him to enter. Here he come....he gazed upon the toys and just like usual, he wanted the one we were playing with. So he scurried over and begin to try to take it, and there it was the jaws of death. He sunk his teeth down on my tricep and I felt the pain begin to set in. I tightened my fist and rared back as far as I could go. Wham!!! Right in the kisser! I had belted him so hard his nose was bleeding and I think his lip too. I immediately felt horrible. Well as you can imagine the sirens came on and the entire house became chaos. His dad came running. I called him Timbo. He stood above and asked "What happened!" Well as quietly as I could say it I told him I socked him in the mouth. Now I don't remember my dad's face at the time but I can imagine the fear and the second thoughts he was having about our conversation at the time. And the words left my mouth, "Daddy told me too." Even as a small boy I remember thinking I had drastically dramatized this incident. I don't remember what happened after but it would take a whole lot more than that to shake their stone friendship. That kid grew up to be a very smart Badass nurse and medic. His dad over the years from that point would guide me into being a very accomplished hunter as he was a real "mountain man". I learned a lot from him, and I would coerce my sister into drinking his spit bottles a few times, he left laying around......love ya Timbo

My Old Friend

My most bestest friend I've ever had was the coolest guy around. Denton Texas 1992, I was at a little convienece store that was known all around where regardless of age a fella could buy alcohol. I walked in grabbed a case, through it up on the counter and away I went. I was with a couple buddies. As I exited the store I noticed him leaned up against the wall smoking a cigarette. We exchanged pleasantries and I got in my truck. I was the ripe old age of 16. We sat in the parking lot for about 30 min catching a buzz before heading down to the strip to wave at girls. Right before we pulled out the kid came over and asked for a ride. Seemed nice enough, so "Hop in dude!" and away we went. We cruised the strip for hours talking. He was the coolest guy I'd ever met, my friends liked him too. He knew all the witty lines to say to the girls and I remembered thinking I want to be just like this guy. As the night wound down, I told him were headed back to our town, where should we drop ya? He replied awww just drop me outside of town somewhere, I'll walk home. So we did. A few weeks later I ran into him again after a football game we had. He was hanging out by my truck after we all showered and cleaned up. He asked what I was up to and if I wanted to hangout, Sure I said. We spent the rest of the night at a bonfire outside of town getting drunk and hangin with friends. Talked for hours about where he grew up and how he was homeless and didn't have friends. I couldn't help but think of how this couldn't be true, everyone liked him and wanted to be around him. So we became as thick as thieves. Soon I had to ship off to bootcamp and we had to say our goodbyes. I tried to talk him into going into the military with me, but he said no. So off I went on my adventures. We exchanged phone numbers and I said I'll write you everyday. After I was stationed in Hawaii for a bit all I could think of is him and wished we could hangout here. So one day we made plans and saved up some cash and flew him out. The island was not ready for the duo. We partied just like in high school. We hit all the clubs. I had to find a way for him to stay. So after a long talk with the misses, we moved him in. She loved him too. I mean who didn't, he was amazing. Soon our friendship became strained with a kid on the way and all the partying. So he packed up and went back to Aubrey TX. I never missed anyone as much as him. We would end up having a few reunions from time to time and eventually ended up living really close in Louisiana. It was on again, like we had never been apart. If you seen him you seen me, and vice versa. We got in alot of trouble and had some amazing adventures. He also loved to fish and hunt as much as I did. We continued our connected at the hip relationship for years. I had a grandpa that also had a best friend that they were always seen together and I would think how cool would it be to have a friend like that. We weathered alot of broken hearts and hard times together. We seen alot of hurt, death, and broken friendships. I could do anything with him by my side. I didnt make any decisions without him, some were made because of him. I would never go where he and I together wasn't welcome. Jump forward many years we begin to have strains on our relationship. He became someone I didn't know. He wasn't that tall lanky kid leaned up against the store anymore. We had ran together for almost 30 years and I was going on a trip. I told him where I was going and for the first time I wanted to go alone. I didn't know how I would make it without him, hell we had conquered the world together. But I knew deep down this was it. We never fought or argued but something deep down said we had to be apart. I ended up driving him to a campsite with me for the last night. Way out in the desert we said our goodbyes and for the first time I wasn't concerned about where he would stay, or how he would find his way. I just knew I had to drive away and not look back at him. Life went on and for the first time I had to make decisions without him. I had to determine what, when, and where I'd go without his help. I realized I didn't know how to talk to people without him, I didn't know how to talk to pretty women without him, I thought to myself "My God, he was the best part of me!" Slowly I begin to learn how to function without my all time bestest friend. "Oh, his name?"......"Alcohol, ...his name was Alcohol....."...alot of people can handle their alcohol, I could not....so when you ask if I want a drink and I say no, don't apologize... it's completely fine....he lives far far away....I know in my heart I'll never see him again.....but the times we had......this was by far my hardest story....

A Tool is Merely a Tool.

I get asked many times a day by prepper folks what is the most important thing to have prepped if everything goes to hell in a hand basket. I'll give ya hint, its not a thing. From an early age I was blessed with a family that didn't use the phrase, " I don't know how". Nobody called a handyman, no one called a plumber, no one called a mechanic. It just got done. I know what your thinking well they were smart and knew how. Well yes they were and did. But who taught them? I remember watching the movie Astronaut Farmer and thinking I'm so glad dad never got the notion to go to space cause he would have went. My oldest uncle probably should have been a professor somewhere in a school for anything. If I asked him how to do something, you weren't given a class to do it, you were given the materials and alot of space to destroy things a few times and you learned yourself. He wasnt being an ass, he was teaching a valuable lesson in that the best tool is your brain, its actually the only tool. You can buy everything, prep everything, but what happens if thats all taken away? Prep your mind...soon you will realize the fear subsides and you realize you are prepped, regardless what you have or where you are, your prepped. If a man had no idea how to write poetry he would need to amass tons of poetry, hide it all, try to keep it safe, worry constantly that someone would steal it....but a poet....he fears not because he is a poet regardless of what happens. Mistakes aren't failed attempts, they are unfinished trys. Get rid of the fear and live.....

Let your receding hair down.

So we have in ways found that I was definitely a wild child and trouble was beginning to become my middle name. Well my junior year in high school things would begin to spill over as I found it harder and harder to stay out of trouble. My high school was in a small farm town. It was a time right on the edge of change. School shootings hadn't became a thing yet. Most of us had rifles or shotguns in gun racks in our truck back glasses in the parking lots at school, and would sometimes clean guns in AG class. We would have kids transfer from bigger city's who were very disrespectful to the teachers and the the local kids would deal with them after school. We would cut up and get in trouble but you were never disrespectful to the teachers because all the families in town knew one another and it was just something that didn't happen. Most of my teachers were teachers when my mom & uncles was there as a student. One day after school one of these kids had said some things about my mom who worked in the school. So I dealt with it accordingly, I rearranged his braces in his mouth for him. It just so happened that we had got a new principal in school that was also from one of the bigger cities. Alot of folks were having problems due to his style of disciplinary actions. Well the next day I showed up at the office to face the music of the previous days actions. I had gotten "paddlings" alot when I was in school, in fact I chose them over detention because well lets face it, my dad knew how to paddle and these so called licks in school were a joke in comparison. Now I dont know what this man was going through or if he was just simply having a bad day, but as I entered the office he grabbed me by the neck and proceeded to bend me over his desk. My own dad didn't even put his hands on me like this so I proceeded to show him where his chair was made sure he stayed in it. Welp I thought this is it for me now, I'm done with school. So I told the receptionist "I Quit!" And off I went. To make a long story short I dropped out and enrolled into a special school for kids that got in trouble alot but they also had another system installed where if you could pass a test, you could basically test out of all your classes. I hated school work but I wasn't a dummy by no means. I had just taken the assessment test to go into the military and scored so high they were going to give me $8k in signing bonuses and choose my career path. So this was perfect for me, hell I'll test out of all of them and graduate in 2 weeks. And I did. Now halfway thru this my truck had broken down and I was living my grandfather at the time. He was very well mannered man and didn't ever do anything out of the norm. He was highly respected around town. He seldom swore, if he did it was the word Hell but that was it. He didn't drink either. Very quiet. On occasion I could get him to open up and tell some war stories from WW2 when he stormed the beaches. He had sold his truck and got a small antique car. I would think to myself, he looks so funny driving that tiny car with his cowboy hat on. I was at that age where just about everything was embarrassing and he was going to have to take me and drop me off in front of all these "bad" kids at high school. I cringed at the thought. So we did and I couldn't get out of the car fast enough. I spent the whole day worrying about him filing up the big half circle drive and park in front to pick me up, in front of the entire school getting released for the day. I had knots I my stomach just thinking about it. Looking back now I know he was worried about me and was doing everything in his power to get me graduated and off to bootcamp before I messed it all up and ended up in jail or something. I tried to time it so I could get outside before the majority of kids made it out but as I came out he was right there in front in that old car. Oh I thought this is horrible. So I crawled in and we sat patiently, well he did, I couldn't wait for the line of trucks and nice cars to get out of the way. As it became our turn, the crowd of kids had amassed right beside us. The big truck in front gave out a loud diesel bark and spun the tires as the cool kids sped off. I have no idea what was going through my grandfather's mind at the time but I guess he felt the situation and was going to lighten the mood. Out of nowhere he stepped on the gas pedal all the way to the floor. The old cars engine came alive and the smoke begin to bellow from the back tires, it was slow to take off due to the rear tires spinning freely but as it did I watched him turn the wheel towards the grass of the courtyard and away we went. Right out into the Grass of the courtyard and begin cutting doughnuts right there in front of the entire school. You could hear the entire crowd cheering as he threw grass and dirt all over the place. Around about the 3rd doughnut he corrected it and away we went down the street with a huge cloud of burnt rubber smoke followed. He gave out a short giggle and said I haven't done that in years. I didn't even know what to say. He got to see me graduate and got to see me sign my military entry papers and passed away a week later leaving his friends coffee hangout at Dairy Queen in the parking lot in that old car. I would cut my left leg off with a dull knife to sit in that car with him again.....

Our memory's are jaded.

I was about to start first grade and I really enjoyed school because where we lived out in the country, there werent any kids to play with close by. My birthday always fell a few weeks after school started. For the past year or so I loved, craved, and wanting everything G.I.Joe. my grandmother on my moms side always mailed my gift really early before my birthday and it was always wrapped. I had asked for a few things but this size and shape box wasn't lining up with anything I had ask for. What was it I thought to myself. I was a pretty good kid and didn't get in alot of trouble on purpose that is. My kind of trouble came from accidents and things that weren't foreseeable to me. Ya know bad decisions. My mother and dad worked during the day and back then I stayed by myself at home. It was only for a few hours but it was the norm back then and for the area of South Texas. I would sit for hours picking up the box and moving it around and was completely oblivious to what it could be. So I began to build up the courage to attempt to open a small corner to get a glimpse. So I eased a piece of tape back slowly and carefully not to tear the paper. She had really wrapped it good. But I was able to get a corner open just enough to see the familiar colors of the G.I. Joe products. Now my curiosity was growing intense because I still couldn't place which toy this was. I was dieing now. So I began opening the rest very carefully and figured I could put it right back the way it came and noone would be the wiser. After a precision surgery I had successfully removed the box. It was a bright shiny jet. I was on top of the world. Now the way I see it noone will know if I take it out and play with it for a short bit and put it back in the box. It was an amazing toy. So after playing for awhile I cleaned it up and put it all back together. You couldnt tell I had ever touched it. I continued to do this daily as my birthday grew closer. Then I had to practice being excited and surprised so my foolproof plan would work out to the last detail. It went off with out a hitch. Fast forward a bit to my 16th birthday. My mom had created a scrapbook with all the photos she had taken throughout my childhood, it was so cool, she even had wrote stories to go with the photos. So thumbing through it one afternoon I came to photo that looked as if she had photographed a piece of garbage. So I took it to her and asked what it was. She replied, "That's the present you opened everyday before your 6th birthday." I was like, seriously? She continued to explain to me that her and dad would laugh and talk about it each day as the wrapping paper got worse and worse. Eventually towards the end she said we couldn't even tell what the wrapping paper looked like and more of the toy was showing then was covered. It was my first inclination as to what we perceived as a child was not as we perceived when were grown, the jets wing was broken, it had dirt all over it and most of the pieces were missing. I stuck with my story.......someone obviously broke in and done that.....

Highway to Hell

So we remember "M" from previous stories. M, me, and her kids from a previous marriage and 1 dog all lived together on base in Ft Polk Louisiana. M was 16 yrs older than me. We got along super if we were sober. I had papers for transfer to Fort Richardson Alaska, my dream come true. I had dreamed of living there my entire life. I had just recieved my Sargeant stripes so the money to move was much better. A lady at the finance office informed me that if we drove the military would foot the bill and if we budgeted everything on way could stand to have a couple grand leftover. Well this was right up my alley. We could see the country all the way to Bellingham Washington where we drive onto a ferry with a cabin for the family and cruise all the way to Haines Alaska. Then drive the rest of the way. First issue was it was the dead of winter. I dont care, I told myself, this was a chance of a lifetime. Second issue, I owned a 1984 K5 diesel blazer. These were the bread and butter for the time for offroad except mine had 320,000 miles on it when the speedo quit probably in the 80s. Still did not deter me, I could fix anything. So we finalized the paperwork, packed the luggage and away we went. First stop, my parents house. My mom didn't hold anything back in her feelings for M and how she despised her, mainly because she thought she took me from my first wife. Not true. So while we visited, I tried to stay close to M because if mom got the opportunity she would corner her. Well she did anyway, it was bad. M had a heart of gold and loved me to death. So we canceled plans to spend the night because I felt horrible for M and how mom talked to her. I knew this was gonna be hard on dad because he only had a brief moment to see me. So next stop Oklahoma City. My God the wind blew so hard I thought we would loose our luggage on top the roof rack. The rest of the trip went off without a hitch. We finally boarded the ferry and begin to sail. The views from the ship were so beautiful. So we got to the port and unloaded. We were all in shell shock when we got off the ferry because it was a winter wonderland and soooo cold. We were told in Haines Junction, the next leg was long and there were no fuel stops along the way, so I filled the 3 5 gallon spare tanks in the back. We now had enough diesel to burn half the nation's grasslands. Away we went. The drive through the mountains was something out of a national geographic magazine. The roads weren't to bad until we got up in elevation. I had chains but decided we didn't need them just yet. Bam! We hit a spot of black ice. Wasn't to horrible I just slid off the road a bit. Didn't even loose momentum. We continued on for about 3 minutes when I begin to smell something burning. So I quickly begin to pull over, but before I could get it slowed down smoke begin to pour from underneath the dash. It was black thick smoke. My first thought was to get my family out then worry about the truck. There was no shoulder due to the snow plows only cleared the lanes of traffic. So I got it stopped and immediately started helping everyone out. I told M to take them as far as possible due to tanker load of diesel we were hauling. As I lifted the hood, the flames were intense. They were bellowing well over the hood and windshield. I noticed the transmission line to the radiator had been snagged and broke and was spraying on the hot manifold. No chance to save her just had to slowly back away and watch her burn. We hadn't seen a car in over 4 hours. So I told M we would remain with the vehicle until the warmth subsides then move to shelter. I knew no one would be able to get around the burnt heap that lay in the middle of the highway. Everything our clothes, keepsakes, it was all gone. M constantly tried to reassure me it was all material things and we were all safe. A Canadian Mounty had seen the smoke and came and picked us up. The fire burnt so hot, there was nothing left of the truck but a pile of ashes and the engine block. To be continued....

The exorcist

My sister came along the day after the fourth of July. How could I forget, I mean I missed all the fireworks action. As mom got closer to the day, I began to realize I was going to have to share the attention of my parents. I had enjoyed being an only child for almost 7 years. I was super excited all the same. Finally somebody I could play with on my adventures. I had it all planned out in my head. The day came, I dont remember why I wasn't allowed in the hospital at the time but dad walked to the window outside of their room and the nurse brought her to the window. She was so tiny and perfect. Love at first sight. I would protect her, make sure she had everything she needed, we would be best friends. Oh how I was wrong, this cruel world will take everything you love if you let it, regardless of who's to blame, it can all go like the switch of a light. Before the world and all our sordid decisions would tear us apart, we were sidekicks. I enjoyed showing her everything from toys to making her listen to dads old vinyl records. I could make her laugh, and cry. She would, without realizing it yet, be the first human to physically knock me out cold. As time progressed the farm duties still had to be maintained so while dad was earning cash we needed, mom would hold down the farm. It got extremely hot and humid on the coast of Texas in the summers. The cicadas would be so loud you couldn't hear a thing and anything that was flat gave off a mirage. Mom would have me watch my sister as she went along her duties. She slept alot when she was first born, but I would figure out a way to keep her awake so I had someone interested in the things I talked about. She would sit for hours listening to ramble on about aliens talking on the old satellite dish in the yard or how I was gonna marry Bo Derek. Mom would come in for lunch and breastfeed my sister. Today was no different, she came in breastfed my sister then we enjoyed some hot sandwiches with melted cheese, my favorite. We finished up and mom was out the door to finish up the chores. As the minutes progressed my sister was extremely agitated. Should would scream bloody murder and then cry. I would walk the house patting her back and she just wouldn't stop. So I decided to maybe use some toys, she loved the fake conversations I made up with my G.I. Joe guys. So I layed her down in her day bed. As I begin to play in front of her to try to take her mind off the screaming she begin to turn weird colors. I was in amazement. She slowly opened her mouth and a stream of white nasty milk shot from her mouth so far and with such force the exorcist would have been shocked. It went up and over my head and covered everything. My parents never stopped me from watching movies that were violent or scary. I did have to turn my head during naked scenes. Looking back I believe that's where I got my vivid imagination from, me and dad loved horror movies. Oh yea back to the demented possession that was now laying in my sisters day bed. She had got a demon in her and it's now my responsibility to inform mom. I ran as fast as I could, out the door and ...wait. I probably should bring her with me, it's along ways to where mom was working. So back to foul creature and away we both went. Across the farm to down where the barn was. Mom was running a weed eater cutting brush down. It was hard to get her attention holding the vial creature, who was still spraying milk like a half crimped water hose. Mom stopped and was mid sentence of yelling at me cause she was suppose to be asleep. So I explained the situation. I was at that age, probably still today, not someone to be trusted on the severity of a situation do to my dramatic ways of telling a story and exaggerating. But half way through it and she sprayed again, now mom was running. She got on the phone and made some phone calls to the most important person you could make back then. You didn't call 911, you didn't call a doctor. You called your mom. Which in this case was my moms mom, my grandmother. She asked of all the details and put all the evidence together and explained the situation. See my mom working out in the heat had got too hot. Her breast milk had went bad during her time working in the heat all day. So my sister got a good healthy dose of bad milk. She was fine after a few hours. My grandmother told her what to do and everything was fine. I still gave my sister space, aliens don't just make themselves known, its gradually over time.

The "Thoughtless Ones"

We are all aware that things we put in our bodies affect us. Different foods, drugs, chemicals etc. Some affect ours differently than others. Way back when, the alcohol I consumed on a Friday night would probably kill a small village of sober people. A line of coke snorted through the nose makes us feel all kinds of things. Back in the gold rush days their were people who roamed the mountains known to many as the "thoughtless ones". I read about them in old books about gold mining. They would just wander around the wilderness, couldn't talk or even acknowledge another person. It was later realized they were suffering from mercury poisoning. See they would make batches of mud and clay filled with tiny gold flakes and they learned they could pour mercury in it and mix it with their feet for awhile and the gold would eventually adhere to the mercury in a ball. Then they would heat the mercury up and the mercury would burn off leaving the gold behind. Most knew that the smoke from the mercury was toxic and stayed away. They didn't realize however the mercury was creeping through their skin in their feet and hands into their brain. So we are all very aware and take extreme caution around things that enter our skin, mouth, and nose, but we should also consider the other 2 that we don't pay attention too. Our eyes and ears. These two are by far way worse than the other 3. These allow things in that change everything about us, and if we're not careful, over time we then feel the need to take the toxic things into our mouths and noses to compensate. Be aware of who you surround yourself with or watch on TV. Their words or negativity can be just like alcohol, cocaine, and mercury, slowly changing us into the "thoughtless ones."......

How long you worked here? I dont.

Being out of the military, I was still craving that rush of adrenaline. An old Army buddy of mine turned me onto an outfit in Mexico that specialized in contract work with South American military and law enforcement. Sounded right up my alley because 90% of my specialized training was jungle operations. So I reached out, spoke with a few recruiters and filled out a few applications forms and was in. It took a alittle over a month to get the travel arranged and paperwork done so I was biting at the bit. When I arrived I was greeted by an old guy at the airport and driven to a small compound just outside of a small southern Mexico town. They were shutdown already for the day, so I walked a mile or so to a local bar. I could speak fluent Spanish so

I felt pretty confident of my surroundings. As I entered the bar there were a few white men at the sitting up against the bar and they turned to look, I immediately knew they were prior service. It was written all over the faces and their body movements. So I approached and they acknowledged me as well. Once you've been around our types for awhile we can spot each other pretty easy. I introduced myself and they did the same. We talked for a few hours about our prior engagements and what was in store for us here. We retired for the evening. 6 am I awoke to the banging of a hammer outside so I got up and was gonna go for a short run until 9am. Once outside the heat almost took my breathe away. So I figured I'd just hang around until I was more climatic to the environment. As I entered the room to meet my new supervisor I could tell this place was just a front for somekind of larger operation else where. It was really rundown, no gun range, no arms room...just really half ass put together. So I greeted my new boss, a small Spanish man about 5'5". He introduced him self using alot of slang and words not taught in Spanish classes im assuming to test my working knowledge, well no harm here I learned Spanish working on horse ranches back in Texas, so I responded with my own slang and he grinned and said sit down. We talked awhile about the operations and the positions that were available. I was offered scout due to my background in which I gladly accepted. See the way I saw it, I was kinda in charge of my own destiny by being in the front plus you always knew what was going on instead of being in the rear and having to wait on radio comes to find out stuff. So a few weeks later I recieved my first briefing and task force assignment. It was a drug raid, well, kinda. See they were strapped in there budget so they tried to do more than one at a time to save on cost, and the others would simply move to a different location in the jungle so intel would have to be regained. We could hit one, secure, leave a small team and hit a second one down the trail before first light and before they had a chance to move. I had spent weeks preparing my gear....you were allowed to use all your own gear, sidearm, and issued an M-4 rifle. I was chomping at the bit. We hit the ground about 4 miles from the first target. We made our way down the first canyon with out much trouble from the bush. The second canyon was thicker and took longer to move and remain quiet. The drug outfits would set out sentries not to engage but to pop flares and run. They seldom would shoot because they were so limited on training. Most were farmers just trying to make some quick cash to feed their families. As we got closer I made the team behind me back off so I could move quite solo as to not get busted by the sentry. I could smell cigarettes a mile away and I smelt a good ole stogey going. I stopped the team for a few min to catch him getting a drag. It looks like a slow beacon in the night. Boom I see him. So I slowly make my way up. I get into position to conduct over watch for the team behind me as they make contact with him. Now I don't know how much experience this kid had at pulling guard but they scared him so bad that when he pulled his flare out it popped and raced toward me like a missile. It hit the brush directly behind me and now I couldn't see anything as my night vision had blinded me. Somebody squeezed off a round and it was definitely a 9 mil. So I assumed it was out team. Still no one had broke radio silence. After you've been around weapons a long time you can hear the difference between what they are when their fired. I wasn't moving until I got some vision back. It slowly begin coming back just as one of the task force team leaders called for immediate extraction. He was rambling on the radio about a man down and it was now that I knew I wasn't dealing with real aces. If a man is down and only one weapon was fired, he either shot himself on accident or his buddies are real dicks. So I slowly made my way up to them because lets face it these guys will probably shoot me at this point. Nothing worse than nervous and scared untrained soldiers or police force. As I got to the area. The flare guy had a buddy and he shot the team leader almost center mass chest. He had a vest on but he wasn't gonna be hanging out at the water bottle in the break room any time soon. I asked why are we calling medivac, there's no way a bird is coming anywhere near here with this canopy. I told them we need to continue on to the target which is probably vacant by now, this dude is gonna be fine. They weren't to excited about it. But as the scout I was in charge of movement, now they could make the call to scrub the operation but I said where and how we go. So after walking about another 20 meters or so I thought to myself. Please be vacant because if we get in a fire fight I'm running all the way back to the compound, because these guys don't have a chance and their probably gonna shoot each other. As I got close to the target given to use by the informant, I could feel that good ole friend of mine, adrenaline. I had to find the target before my task was complete and let the band of misfits carry out their mission. I could smell smoke so I knew I was close. It was really quiet which meant they were either ready for us or gone. I was hoping gone. Slowly I begin to move forward and I could make out a large white barrel looking object halfway covered by a dark blanket, yes I'm done I thought to myself. I radioed the team forward and pulled the new team leader up and pointed to him what I had found and told him to go back and come in from the higher ground for better advantage incase they lay wait. As he turned to move his team out the jungle awakened to the sounds of small arms fire. Well here we go I thought to myself. I realized for the first time in my life I was with men I didn't trust to be in this kind of action. In the time it took them to get ready to return fire and engage it was over. They had fled, they had just shot a bunch of rounds off to buy them some time to move out. When we finally got back to my outfit we had a long talk on who I was going to be assigned with from here on out. I missed the trust, brotherhood, and camaraderie of the military. I was in a whole new game now.....

Topgun horse breaking

At some point in my life I learned how to turn my emotions off and refocus pain or hurt somewhere else. Maybe by writing and reading these events we'll learn together what it was. When high school crushes would dump me it was like the whole world was ending. Nowadays it's more like the movie Heat, I don't get attached to anything I can't up and leave in 60 seconds. I enjoyed summers because I could just run free. I was 13 when my first true heartbreak came along. I first noticed here outside my window. We lived on alittle farm that faced a country highway that seen more farm implements than traffic. My window was directly toward the highway. I don't remember what I was doing but I caught her riding her horse down the shoulder of the highway and she was beautiful. She was not the horse. I watched her until I couldn't see her through the window and then ran outside to follow her with my peepers until she was too far to see. I thought to myself, where was she from. Was she just visiting family, did she move here. The mystery drove me crazy. I dont remember how long it was between out next encounter but I caught her again, except this time she was headed the opposite direction. So 2 and 2 together and I knew she was heading in the direction of where she was staying. Did she ride everyday and I just missed the other times? So I gave chase just in the treeline so she couldn't see me. Maybe just maybe I could find the house where she was at and that would give alittle more evidence as to her details. I knew pretty much everyone in a 5 mile radius. She got to the creek crossing and disappeared. Wait, how did I lose her? Back to the house I went. I needed a plan. She obviously likes horses. I have a horse. Were meant to be together. I don't remember when I begin to like girls, honestly I don't ever remember a time not liking them. Seems as if I had a crush each school year from kindergarten. Ok focus, yall are distracting me, where was I...oh yea, horses. My horse was a gentle giant and would do anything I asked of her as long as she was in the mood. On a rare occasion she just wasn't gonna do anything. I hated the work of putting a saddle on so I had grown acustom to bareback. So I figured if I tied up Miss Penny at the gate for an hour or so a day, I was bound to catch her riding and I would just slip up beside her and say hi. Now if you hadn't been paying attention in the rest of the stories I'm am crippled with shyness. So this sounds all well and good in my head but I knew deep down this would probably never work. So the next day I tied ole girl up at the gate, she was a bitch to catch sometimes. As I walked back to the house I noticed my dad was home really early from work. So I slipped over to find out why. He had asthma pretty bad and was having a flare up so he called it a day. My mom was working in the front yard so we were all just kinda hanging out and I caught her out of the corner of my eye. There she was. I sprang into action. I made my way around the back of the house because I didn't want her to see me and assume I was just riding over to say hi. I wanted it to look like I was also riding and caught up to her. My town was known for really expensive race horses and we were just middle class farmers so that was my first task to find out what type of girl she was. This could be found out by her riggin. Saddles told a whole about the financial situation of the rider. I really needed her to be just a country girl if we were to be married. See I always had the big picture in mind. As I got on my horse I thought to myself well she'll definitely know my financial situation cause I was shoeless and shirtless in shorts. No saddle, just a string bean of a kid on a big horse. So I trotted out to the highway and made the turn towards her. She was about a half mile out ahead of me. So I gave ole Penny a kick and off we went. I don't know why the God's were always against me in my early years but it almost felt as if someone was trying to sabotage everything I did. Penny had a knack for getting her bridle off with a post in the fence and at some point tied up had got it halfway off. So as we gained speed I begin to rein her in to slow her down and the brindle came off and now was under her neck and the bit was jingling something fierce against her chest. She didn't like it and we begin to accelerate. Regardless of the plans I had for this lady to marry me and have kids and move to Alaska and become hunting guides, I currently was more focused on not dieing. Penny bad broken the sound barrier just before we passed my princess to be, and there was no slowing down in sight. As we passed her, her horse spooked and just about tossed her. But she had more time and mental cognitive behavior to prepare for her ride then I did so she regained control almost instantly. I on the other hand was trying to stay awake due to the g forces I was being subjected too. Now if you've ever rode horses before your probably aware of their inability to make quick decisions in surprise situations like a really overgrown ditch and culvert coming out from under the edge of the highway I was now coming up on. Being bareback your only means of holding on are 2 fists full of mane hair and the sheer strength of your feet to squeeze the horse with. As Penny seen the ditch she tried to stop and realized that wouldn't work so last minute jumped it. Now that was great for her. For me? Oh no I had ejected as she planted that first foot to stop. See she was mid flight over the ditch. I was above and just out front of her still in the same position I was in while I was on her. As I came into the really tall grass subsonic, I hit and begin rolling but all I could think of was the 1/2 ton bolt of lightning I had just left and where she was going to reenter this situation. As I came to sliding halt I thought to myself here come the hooves. And there they were. She stepped just beside me and away she went. Now I could have broke my spine in 4 places but I was still gonna get up and play this off. She is not gonna purchase a home with a guy that's a pansy. So I sprang up, dusted myself off, dug the grass from my teeth and begin walking towards my horse who was clearly in the next county by now. As the girl approached she asked if I was OK and asked I wanted to ride with her to go fetch my horse. Now there was a million answers I could have have came up with but what's ole slick say? "Nah, happens all the time. I'm breaking horses for my dad." She had the audacity to laugh at me and ride off. My first heartbreak.....

One of these isn't like the other.

This is a very recent memoir I had today. Most of you know I like to camp way out in the middle of nowhere, far away from others. No roads, no trails, no campground. Just raw nature in all its glory. A problem I've always had as a nomad is and will always be, I'm not shitting where I eat. I will NEVER #2 in my rig. Or by my rig in a handy dandy tent. I enjoy a good shovel, wipes, and some cartoons on my tablet, while enjoying a good sun rise or sun set like we done since the dawn of time. I've never been a good shopper. I always over spend or get things I don't need and I hate getting stuff that is expensive. I prefer wipes over toilet paper so I buy nature safe ones. I just so happened on one of these shopping trips in this big town of Santa Fe New Mexico. I was in a hurry cause I hate being in stores too long. I don't remember why I had stopped at Big Lots but I believe it was because I was doing laundry next door. So I grabbed some things and away I went. One of these items was wipes. Fast forward a few days and a few miles, I had picked an amazing camping spot up in the high desert with the most amazing sunsets a fella could see. Got my new pack of wipes, my shovel, my hand soap and my tablet and off I went. I won't bore you with the details in-between but I will just say this. Make damn sure you don't get acne medicated wipes for the unmentionables. Im fairly certain I damn near started a wildfire. The hell with your trending one chip pepper challenge...I challenge you to give a couple wipes with those bad boys. If I was coordinated enough I would have been dragging my ass through the desert like a dog. Hell I would have tried milk if I would have had some. I walked and sat funny for 2 weeks. I now am a true believer and valued customer of the product called "Dude Wipes", they even package them in a all black wrapper so you can't mistakenly buy the wrong ones. In my defense the package did say cucumber infused......

Pissy Waders, Ahhhh Their Warm..

My life long dream was always to live in Alaska. So when my dream came true at the age of 22, I was on cloud 9. I had got to Anchorage in the dead of winter so I didn't get to adjust, just rip off the bandaid and deal with it. It was bad but I quickly adjusted. As spring came I could hardly control my excitement to fish the salmon runs. I had grew up all over the state of Texas and there wasn't a whole lot that would eat you in the woods. Maybe if you died out there of natural causes, then maybe. So I had taught myself and built up my confidence in dealing with bears. I had only seen one in a zoo once in Ft Worth and thought, gees there are pigs on the Red River bigger than this. So the time came and me and a buddy drove 2 hours north to be in the backcountry away from all the tourists and massive turnouts of locals. We parked the truck and waited on the sun to come up a bit before busting brush to the river. We had some coffee and discussed the newly purchased pistols we bought for the occasion. It was prime bear season as they had just came out of their winter slumber and were hella hungry. I would always try to imagine my first encounter how I would respond. Here it wasnt if, it was when. The sun was just peeking over a ridge as we proceeded to bust brush for about a mile to a great slow bend in the river that we figured would be a prime location. I had worked myself up mentally to a point where there was a bear at every point on the hike. We split up to come out on either end of the bend. Ive always done this whole worst case scenario thing in my mind. I felt good about my courage. I could hear the river running heavy with spring snow melt long before we came out of the thick undergrowth on to the bank. As I got closer, the rocks got bigger and more smooth from the huge floods from spring thaw. As I broke through I exaggerated my noise to alert anything of my presence as to not spook anything that might be close. The river was so amazingly beautiful. I could have thrown a rock and hit a salmon with every throw. I thought to myself no one will be as lucky as we will today. I was in such a hurry to get my gear ready and hit the water. Due to the rivers height it was necessary to wade out a bit to get away from the vegetation to cast. I could feel the sharp harsh cold through the waders I had on. It was frigid, probably still below 32° and only thawed because of the swift movement. Being there early and not seeing any wildlife severely spoiled my bravery because nothing could have prepared me for what was about to happen. Now I know your all thinking, here comes a grizzly. Well your all wrong. It was like the doors of a subway train opened during the morning commute. A massive grizzly seemed to walk out of the brush every 30 feet and on both sides. I was livid. I couldn't even breathe. I had mentally prepared myself to deal with one bear not 12. All I could think of is this pistol is just gonna piss off this whole crew. My attention was focused on the bear directly in front of me on the opposite bank, about 20 feet away. It was enormous. It's back was almost the same height as the top of my head. Her head was the size of large beach ball. Her gums hang low with slobber. It was about knee deep in the water just staring at me like some kind of old western stand off. If I backed away would there be one just in the brush waiting for me. I had one on my left about 20 feet away and one on the right about 40 feet away. Then it happened. 2 of the tiniest, cute cubs begin to show themselves behind the huge beast to my front. I thought "Oh my God, I'm done for." In the brief moment I begin to back up, it was like she had sent some kind of subliminal message to rest of the others that she now owned the river. They all begin to make their way in opposite directions as I slowly backed up. We all knew she was about to go all Mike Tyson on us. I temporarily contemplated just laying down and let the river take me away. It was a brief thought. As I felt the brush behind me she begin to grunt and shake her head. I'm sure me and the other bears were all asking ourselves, "Is it me she's pissed at?" I begin moving limbs to get myself further into the vegetation so I could make my way to the truck, get on a plane and never come back. All I could think about is how many there were and where was the next one. She rose to her hind legs and it was if a Clydesdale horse was rared up in front of me. This was my que to get gone. See a bear stands to take in their surroundings and access the situation. It really was a huge relief. I slowly made my way to the truck and my buddy was already there. I couldn't wait to tell him my story but he had already begin to tell me his. Apparently it was the same all up and down the river. That in my book was a huge "Nope"....Im done. So we went back to base and had some breakfast. It was probably for the best it happened that way. It was like an initiation. Because a few days later we were fishing neck and neck with the bears as if we were all the same species. See the bears were so hungry that all social orders and boundaries had been dropped for the run. The only rule apparently was give the mommas a wide birth. My entire time in Alaska was the most amazing time of my life. And just an FYI, it takes along time to get the smell of piss out of waders.....

Part 2 Highway to Hell

So we left off hitching a ride with the Canadian Mounty back to Haines Junction. This was a small town with a few stores and a small motel. We got a room. Word had spread quick what had happened and people from town begin showing up dropping off clothes, food, blankets, and toiletries. It was the damnedest thing I had ever seen. It was hard to understand a few of them due to the strong accents. A gentleman asked me to come to the bar later and he would buy me a drink and figure out a plan. Well I had a plan. We were gonna catch the local bus that ran all the way to North Pole Alaska, yes it exists. The bus wouldn't be there for about 3 days. The bar was next door so "M" and I went over. The whole bar was so nice and took up a collection for us, which we refused as we had plenty of funds. It was insane how friendly and thoughtful this town was. After having a few drinks too many, my new best friend said he would come by in the am and get me for a snow mobile ride. I had never been on one, hell I'd only seen snow a handful of times in Texas. 7 am came quick, and was still alittle tipsy from the night before and he showed up like an alarm clock. He picked me up, briefly gave me a walk thru on the do's and don'ts. And away we went. We drove all over the country side, across frozen lakes, through the wilderness, up a mountain and back. My hands would take a month to thaw out. The time had come to pack up and catch the bus. I almost didn't want to leave, the town was like a dream. The bus came and half the town turned up to wave us on. How I wished I would have stayed in touch with him, but I was young and had no idea of the importance of those kinda friendships yet. "M" was weary of the stress we had been through so I was hopefull everything else would go off without issue. We spent the next 2 days traveling and finally reached our destination right before Christmas. We recieved our new apartment within hours of arriving which was crazy fast with the military. I got my re-enlistment bonus the next day and we stocked the house. It was a magical Christmas. The kids had a blast learning how to ski on the hill on base and "M" and I turned the basement into our new winter time hangout. The next day "M" wasn't feeling good and had a severe migraine. She had had an aneurysm a few years prior and was worried. We went to the Emergency room to get her checked out. She had a plate in her head from the previous surgery. She ended up just being dehydrated. If I could have only seen into the future.......fuck fate!

See spot run, see spot never again..

My memory of 4 years old is spotty. Seems as if only the dramatic times are engraved. I had a dog named spot. We did everything together, as she was my first dog. I was having trouble at the time and we'll go into that later in Volume 3, of some things that were either happening to me or my mind made up later on its own. So I would spend the days outside with spot while my mom cleaned the neighbors houses. My entire life I've never had a dog that didn't run off all the time. I was jinxed by something apparently. Well spot at least once a week would dissappear for a few days then turn up. Well this day was different. She didn't come home. I was heartbroken. I remember my mom driving around looking for her. This is where my memory becomes spotty. I don't remember how they found out but she had been picked up and put in the pound. So mom told me that we could drive outside of town and see her in the big kennel cage they kept all the strays. So we drove out and it was dark. Dad pulled the car up so the headlights would shine on the fence and she came running. I greeted her through the chain link. Something wasn't right. Why did we come at night and why weren't we taken her home. Mom told me we didn't have the money to get her out and this would be our final goodbye. Now out of everything in my life I've been through, this right here stuck the worst. The nightmares of the light shining on the kennel. See her wag her tail in excitement.....I set here right now in tears thinking about it. Of all the death and misery, homelessness, jail, abandonment, divorce.....this is my worst memory.......

My sweet sweet "M"....

I was fairly accomplished at making bad decisions. I was basically a pro. "M" and I truly believed we were soulmates. We had the best of times. Our downfall was we were both extreme alcoholics. We both would drink til we argued. Make up and repeat like we would never do it again. There was no question that we loved each other. After about 6 years and some of the most best and memorable times we had both come to the realization that we couldn't keep doing this. It was strange that neither one of us ever talked about maybe we should quit drinking and live happily ever after. We had decided to live apart and just be friends. This worked great for about a week at a time. One of us would have too much to drink and we would end up back in bed together. It was like our relationship flip-flopped. Now we were fine as long as we were drinking. "M" finally met someone and he treated her good. So we met at my apartment and made the decision that we couldn't keep up our weekly rendezvous anymore. We still talked about every 3 days on the phone. About 3 weeks later I was in a hotel out of town working and her daughter had called my dad and got my cell number. She called me, I answered and she very slowly and crying told me that "M" was gone. I sat in disbelief as she said she had gotten up for work and was brushing her hair in front of the mirror and fell over. She had a massive hemorrhage in her brain and passed away. Every memory we had had came flooding in. I didn't sleep for 3 days. I didn't go to funeral out of respect for the fella she was with. I went a few days later to say my goodbyes and she was buried right next to her younger brother who she missed so passionately. You will be forever missed "M"......I'll never forget that day, you standing on my porch, in daisy dukes holding a Corona and that giggle.......I need a break now....I'll see yall in Volume 3 thank you so much for tagging along....

Made in the USA
Columbia, SC
22 December 2023